FOR ORGANS, PIANOS & ELECTRONIC KEYBOARDS

E-Z PLAY TODAY 248

The Love Songs of ELTON JOHN

Cover photo: Photofest

ISBN 978-1-61780-397-0

HAL•LEONARD®
CORPORATION

7777 W. BLUEMOUND RD. P.O BOX 13819 MILWAUKEE, WI 53213

Visit Hal Leonard Online at
www.halleonard.com

contents

4 Believe

6 Blue Eyes

8 Can You Feel the Love Tonight

14 Chloe

11 Don't Go Breaking My Heart

18 Don't Let the Sun Go Down on Me

22 I Guess That's Why They Call It the Blues

26 I Want Love

36 I've Been Loving You

40 Little Jeannie

31 Made for Me

Love

44 Michelle's Song

50 Nikita

54 The One

47 Someday Out of the Blue (Theme from El Dorado)

58 Something About the Way You Look Tonight

62 Sorry Seems to Be the Hardest Word

66 Written in the Stars

70 You Can Make History (Young Again)

78 You Gotta Love Someone

74 Your Song

Songs

Believe

Registration 2
Rhythm: 8-Beat or Rock

Words and Music by Elton John
and Bernie Taupin

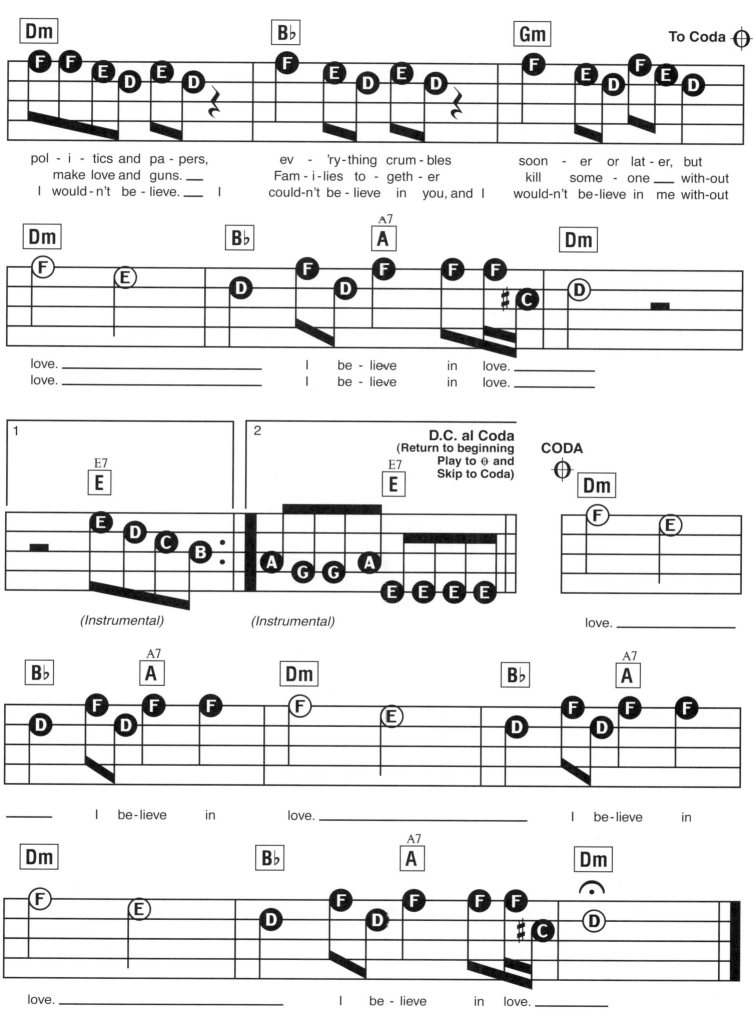

Dm   **B♭**   **Gm**   To Coda ⊕

pol - i - tics and pa - pers,   ev - 'ry - thing crum - bles   soon - er or lat - er, but
make love and guns. __   Fam - i - lies to - geth - er   kill some - one __ with - out
I would - n't be - lieve. __ I   could - n't be - lieve in you, and I   would - n't be - lieve in me with - out

Dm   **B♭**   A7 **A**   **Dm**

love. _____   I be - lieve in love. _____
love. _____   I be - lieve in love. _____

1   E7 **E**   2   **D.C. al Coda**
(Return to beginning
Play to ⊕ and
Skip to Coda)   E7 **E**   **CODA** ⊕   **Dm**

(Instrumental)   *(Instrumental)*   love. _____

B♭   A7 **A**   **Dm**   **B♭**   A7 **A**

____ I be - lieve in love. _____   I be - lieve in

Dm   **B♭**   A7 **A**   **Dm**

love. _____   I be - lieve in love. _____

Blue Eyes

Registration 1
Rhythm: Swing or Ballad

Words and Music by Elton John
and Gary Osborne

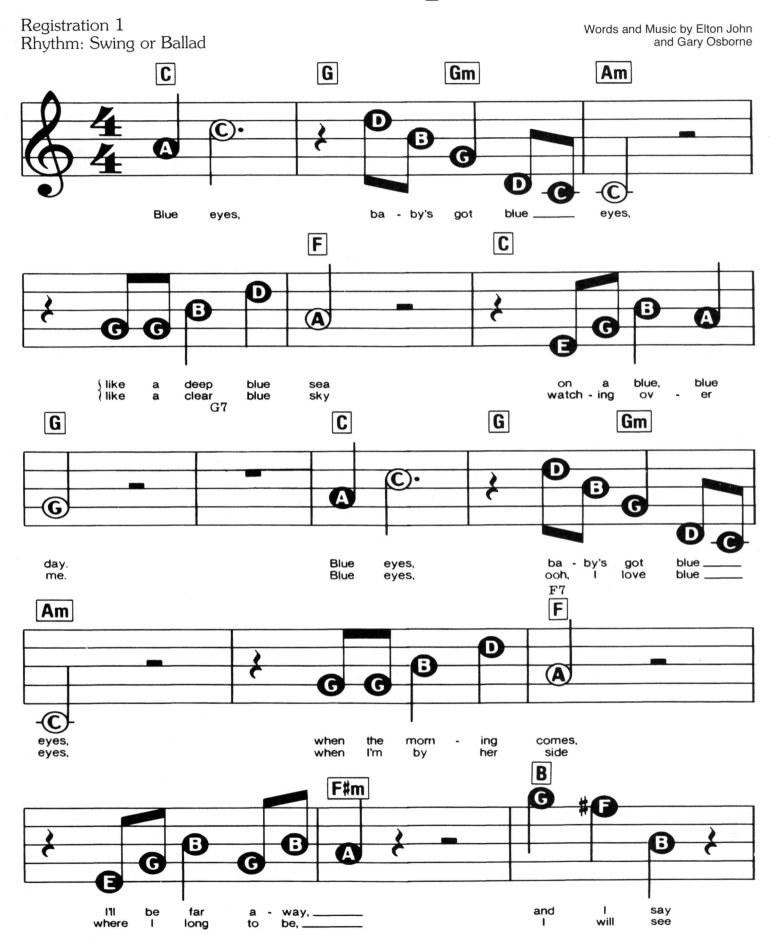

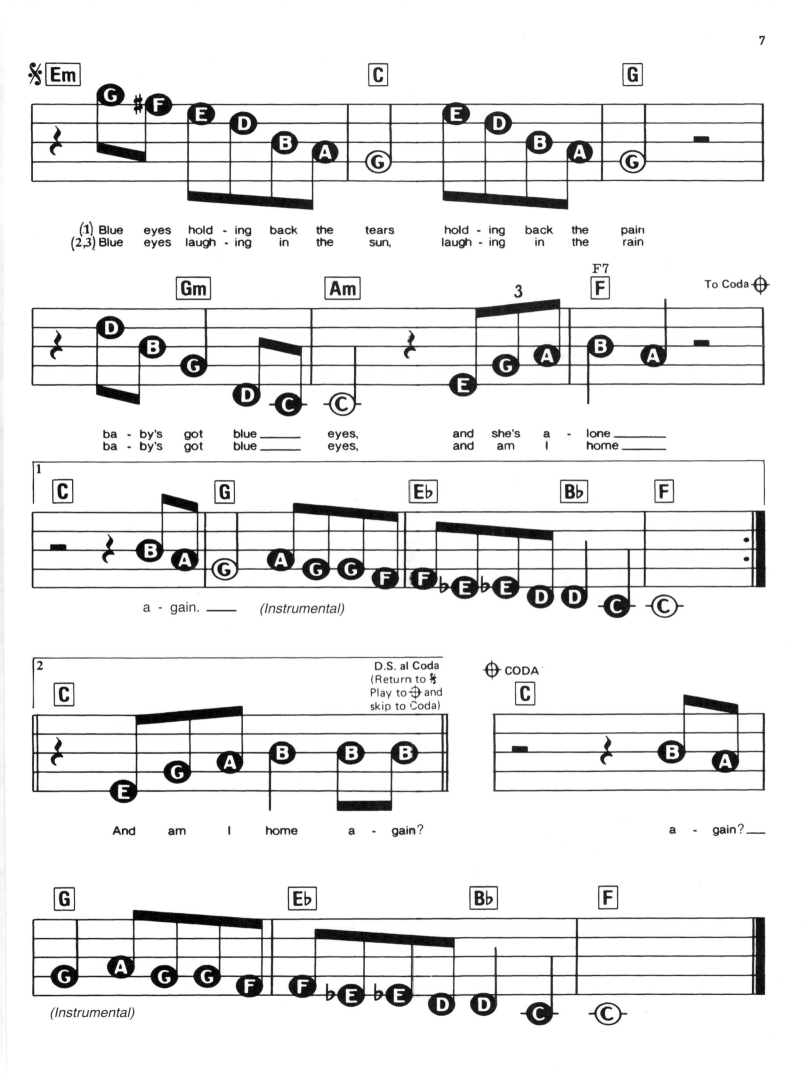

Can You Feel the Love Tonight
from Walt Disney Pictures' THE LION KING

Registration 1
Rhythm: Ballad or Pops

Music by Elton John
Lyrics by Tim Rice

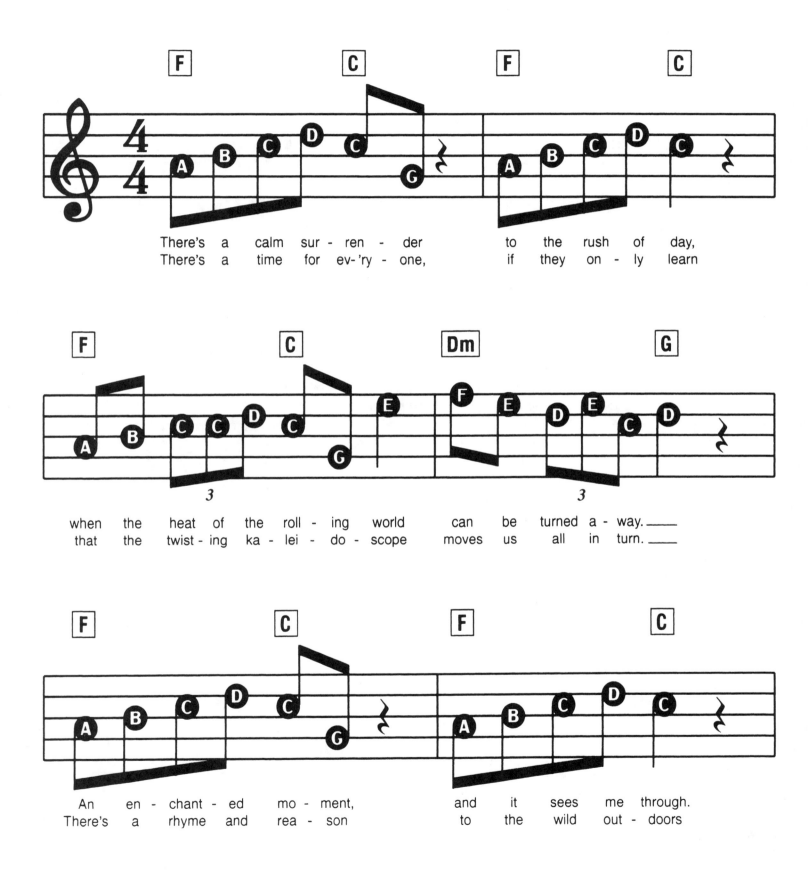

There's a calm sur-ren-der to the rush of day,
There's a time for ev-'ry-one, if they on - ly learn

when the heat of the roll-ing world can be turned a-way.___
that the twist-ing ka-lei-do-scope moves us all in turn.___

An en-chant-ed mo-ment, and it sees me through.
There's a rhyme and rea-son to the wild out-doors

9

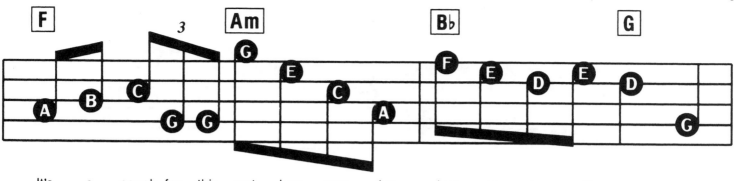

It's e - nough for this rest - less war - rior just to be with you.
when the heart of this star - crossed voy - ag - er beats in time with yours. } And

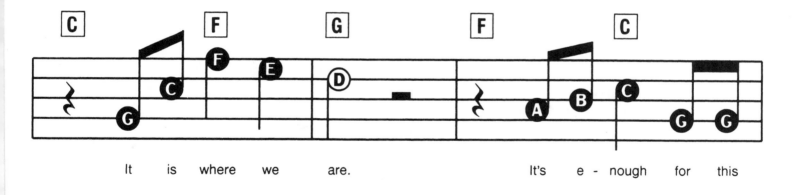

can you feel the love to - night?

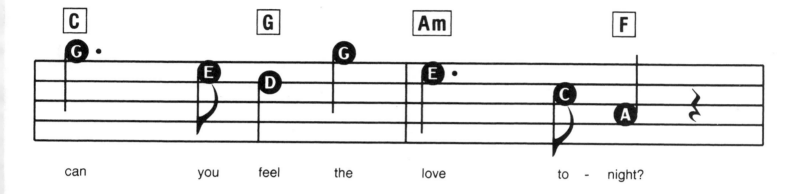

It is where we are. It's e - nough for this

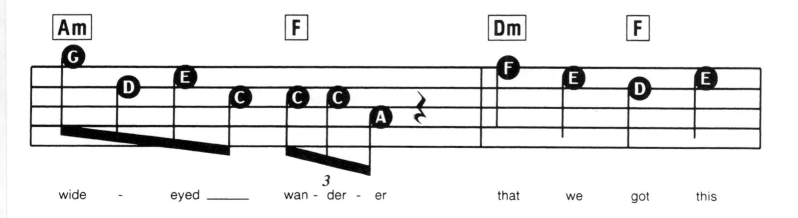

wide - eyed _____ wan - der - er that we got this

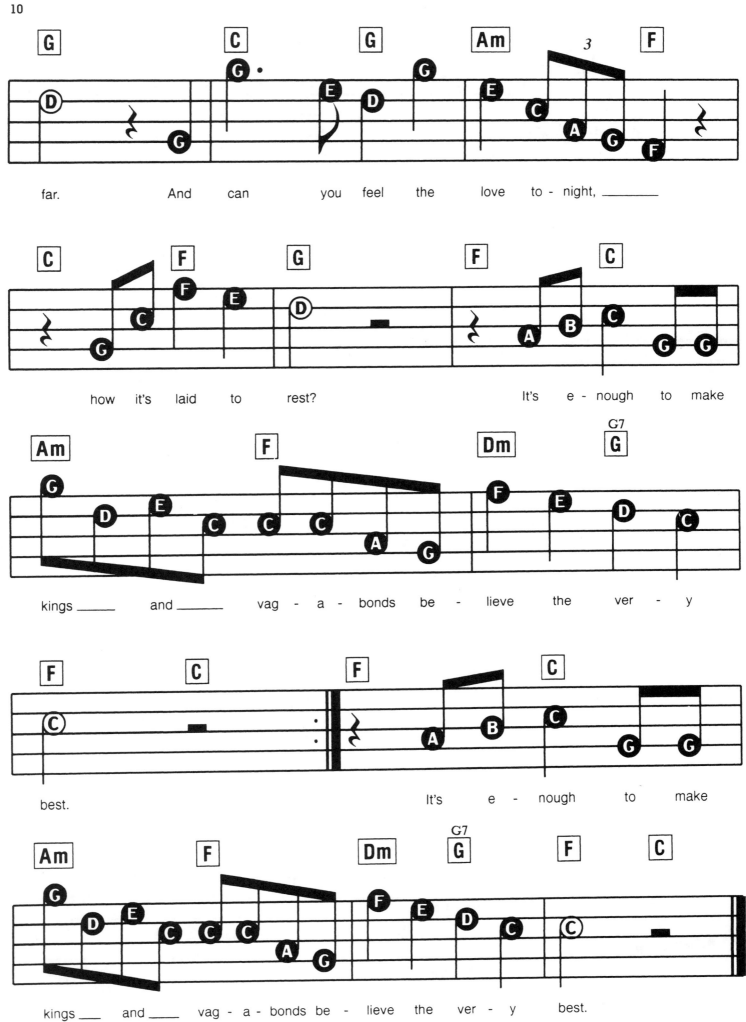

Don't Go Breaking My Heart

Registration 2
Rhythm: 8-Beat or Pops

Words and Music by Carte Blanche
and Ann Orson

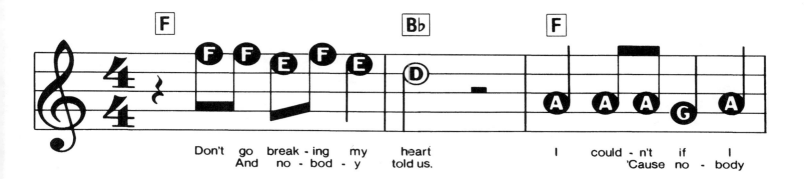

Don't go break-ing my heart
And no-bod-y told us.

I could-n't if I
'Cause no-body

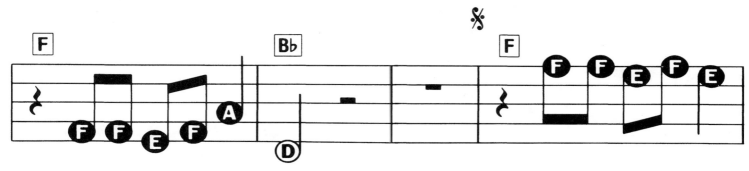

tried.
showed us

Oh hon-ey if I get rest-less
And now it's up to us babe

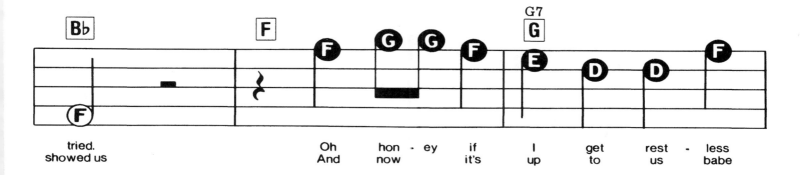

Ba-by you're not that kind.
Oh, I think we can make it.

Don't go break-ing my
So don't mis-un-der-

D.S. (Instrumental)

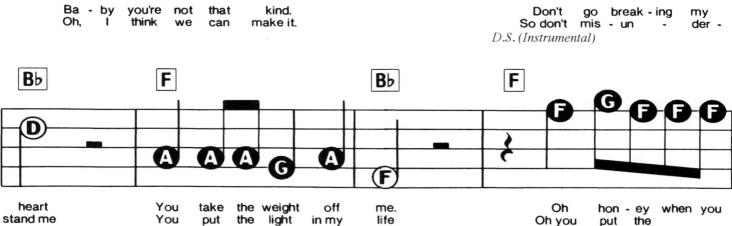

heart
stand me

You take the weight off me.
You put the light in my life

Oh hon-ey when you
Oh you put the

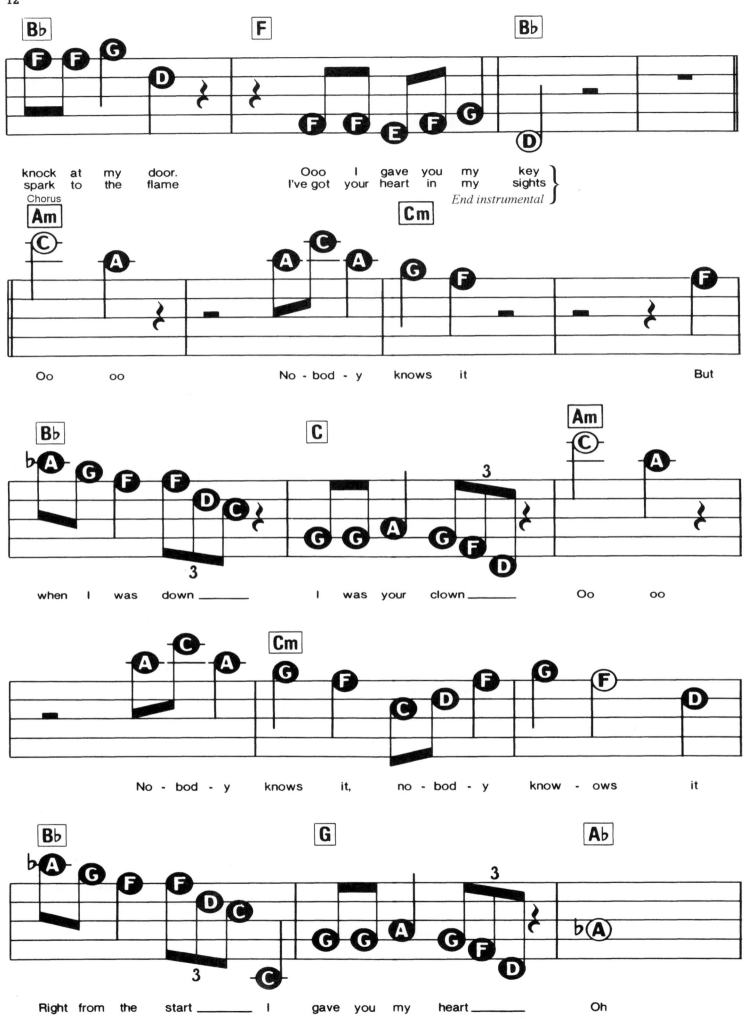

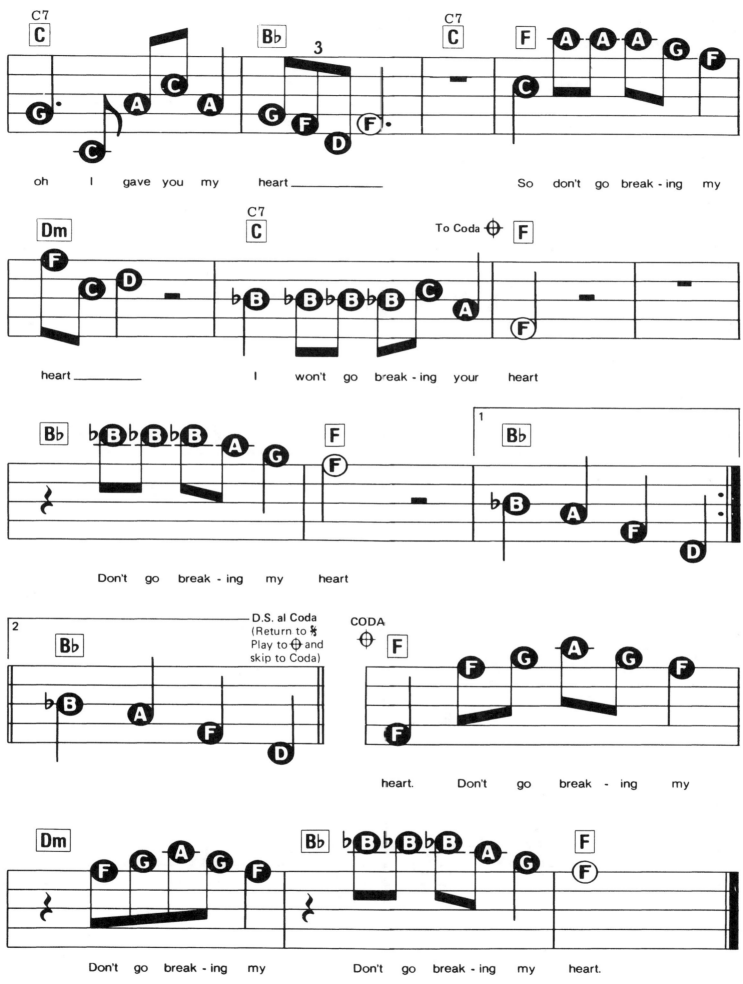

Chloe

Registration 8
Rhythm: 8-Beat or Pops

Words and Music by Elton John
and Gary Osborne

How come you're so un - der - stand - in'_____
How you han - dle what you live through_____
You're the life - line that I cling to_____

when I tell you all my lies, _____
I can nev - er hope to learn, _____
when I feel like giv - in' in, _____

and pre -
tak - in'
when the

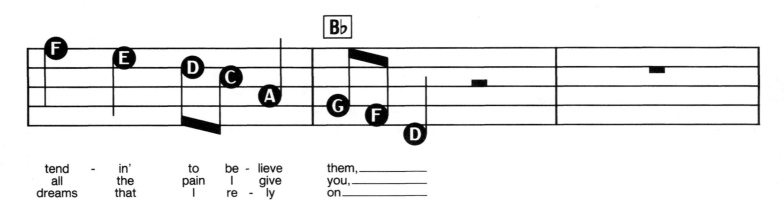

tend - in' to be - lieve them,_____
all the pain I give you,_____
dreams that I re - ly on_____

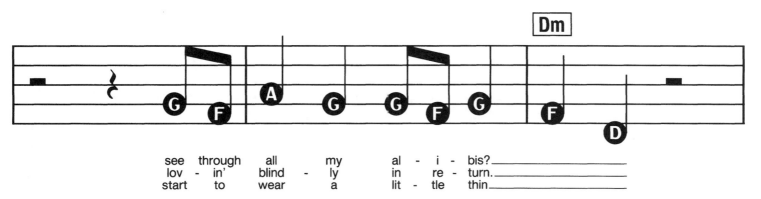

see   through   all   my   al - i - bis?_____
lov - in'   blind - ly   in   re - turn._____
start   to   wear   a   lit - tle   thin_____

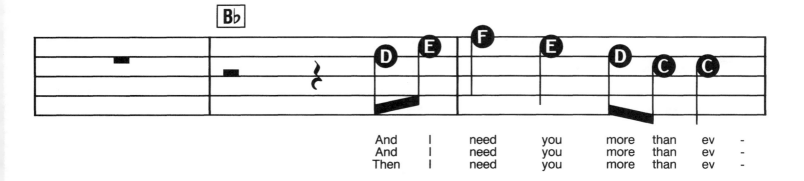

And   I   need   you   more   than   ev -
And   I   need   you   more   than   ev -
Then   I   need   you   more   than   ev -

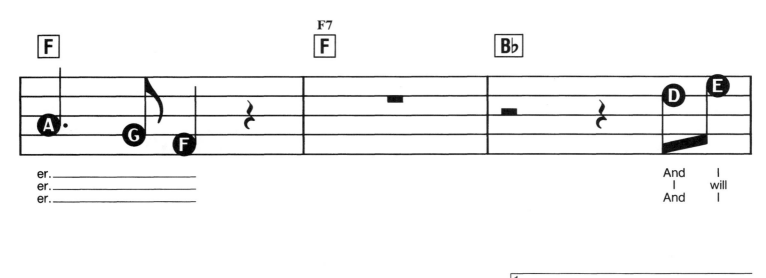

er._____
er._____
er._____

And   I
I   will
And   I

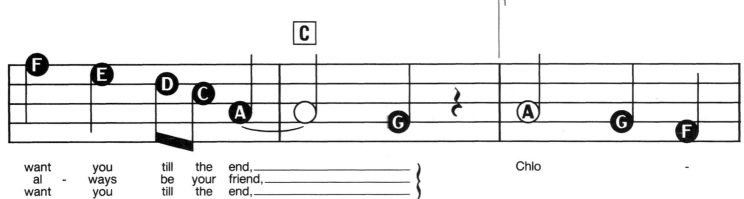

want   you   till   the   end,_____
al - ways   be   your   friend,_____
want   you   till   the   end,_____

Chlo -

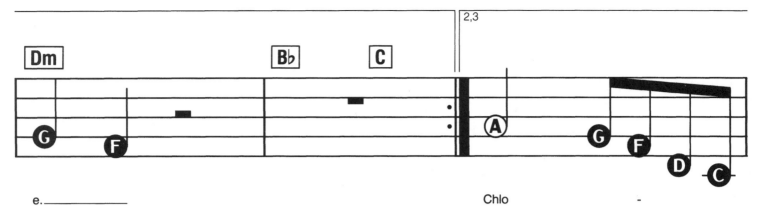

e._____

2,3

Chlo -

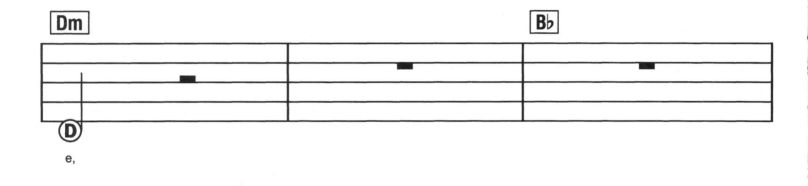

e,

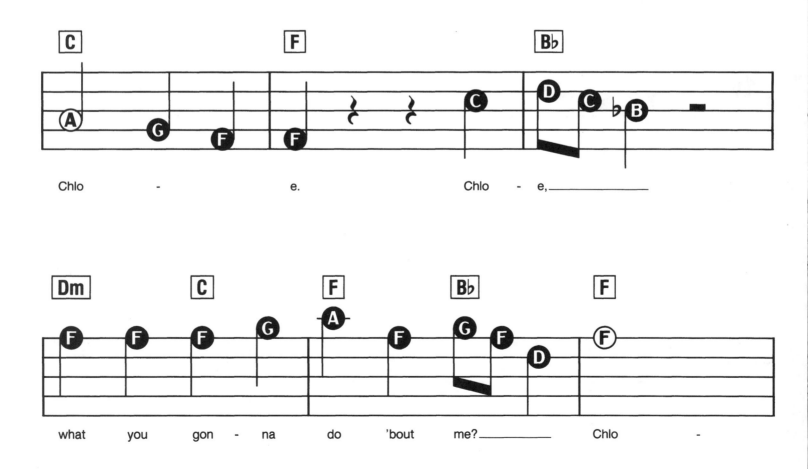

Chlo - e. Chlo - e,_____

what you gon - na do 'bout me?_____ Chlo -

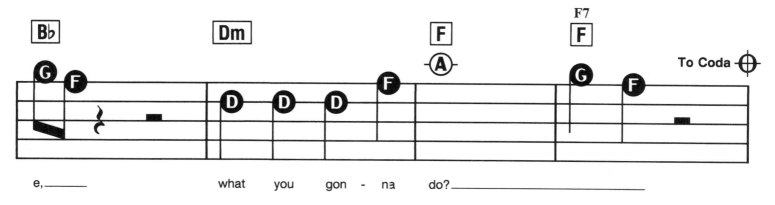

e, _____ what you gon - na do? _____

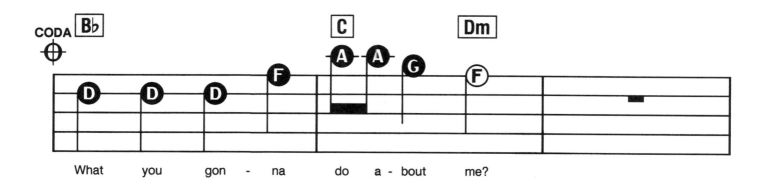

What you gon - na do a - bout me?

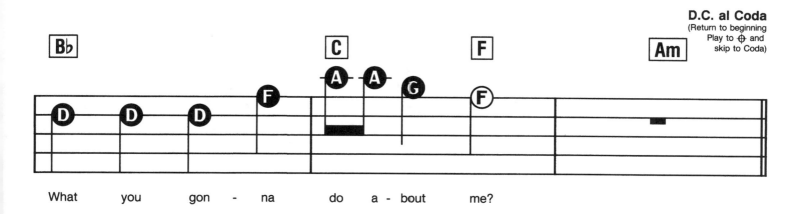

What you gon - na do a - bout me?

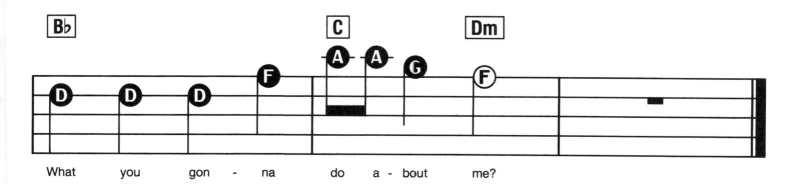

What you gon - na do a - bout me?

Don't Let the Sun Go Down on Me

Registration 8
Rhythm: Ballad

Words and Music by Elton John
and Bernie Taupin

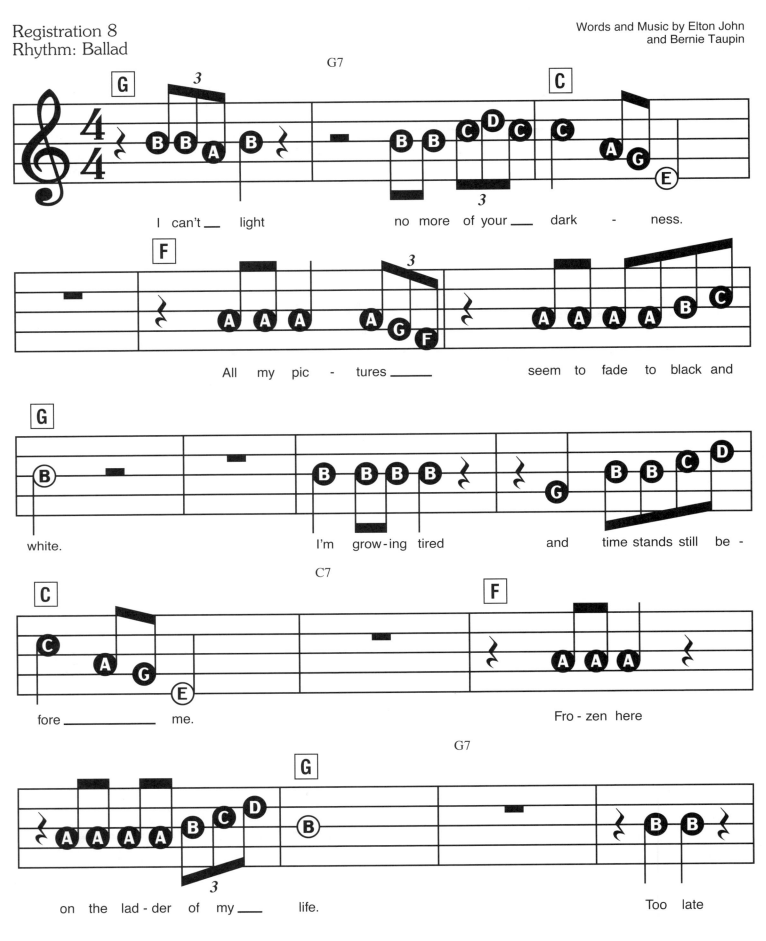

I can't light no more of your dark - ness.

All my pic - tures seem to fade to black and

white. I'm grow - ing tired and time stands still be -

fore me. Fro - zen here

on the lad - der of my life. Too late

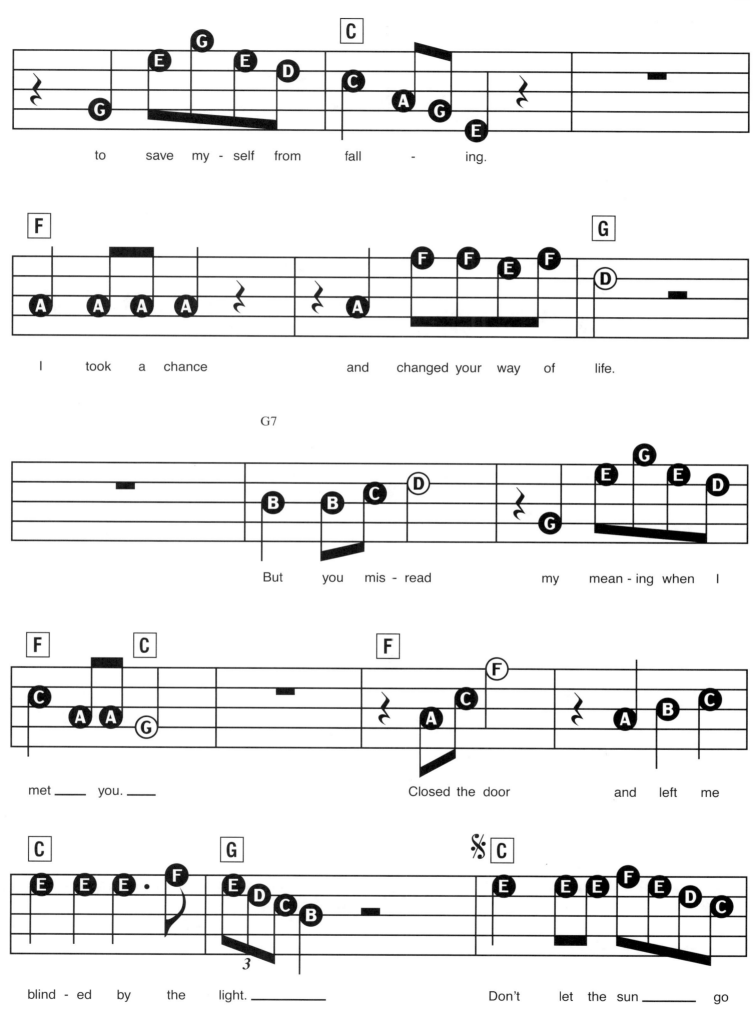

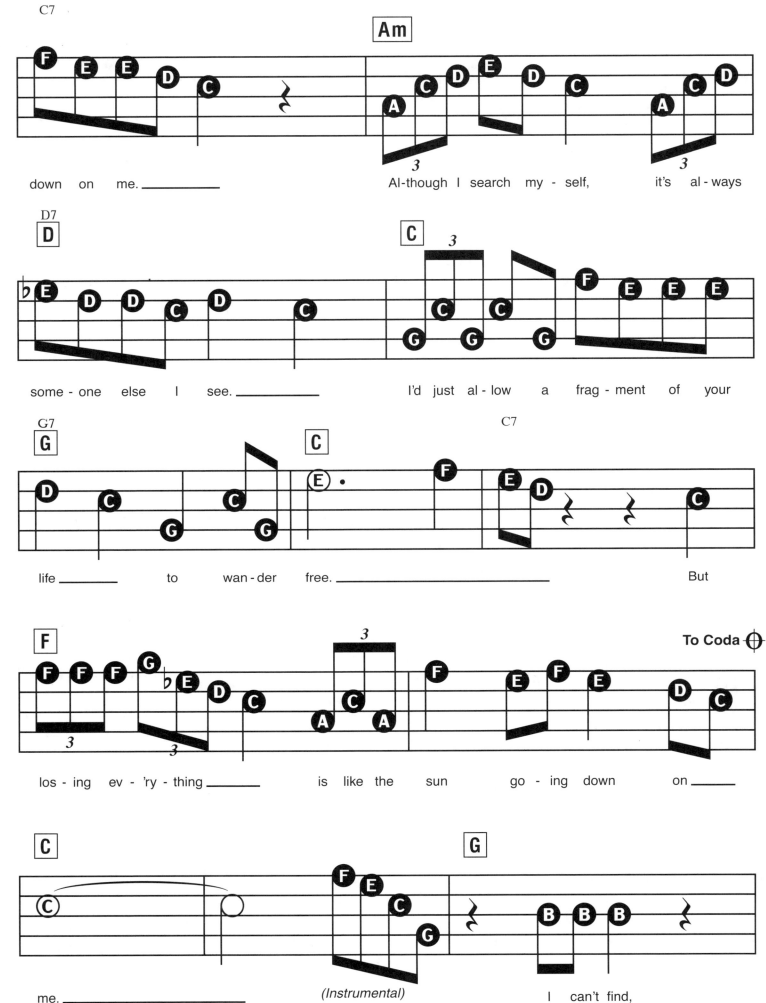

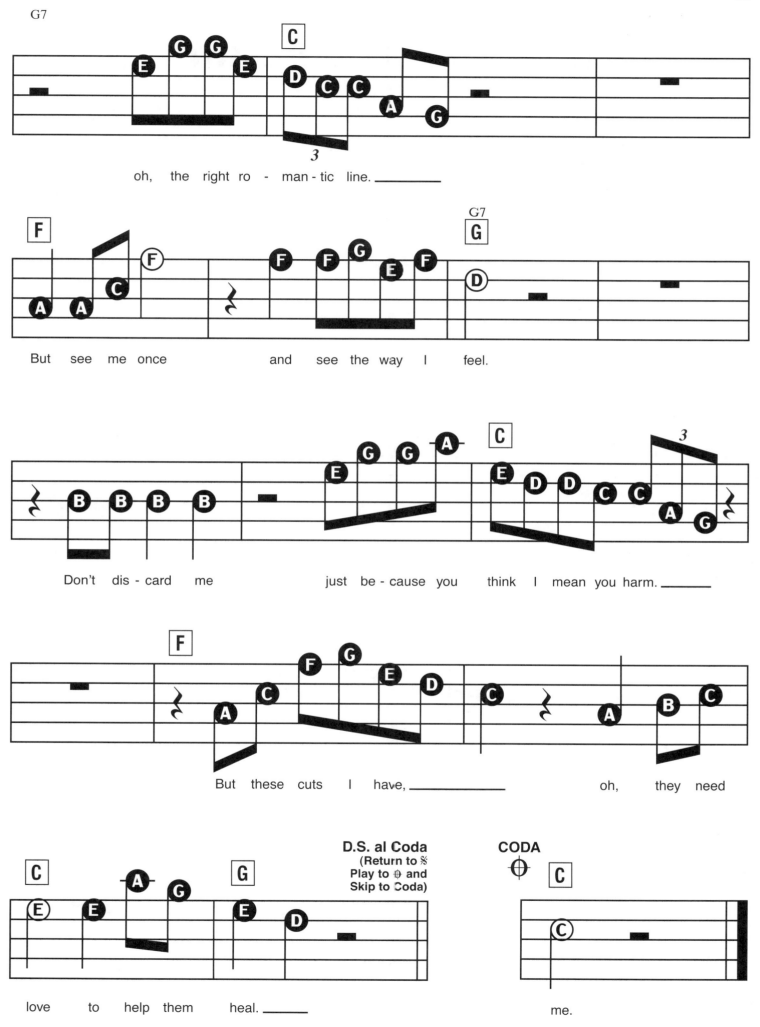

I Guess That's Why They Call It the Blues

Registration 4
Rhythm: Slow Rock

Words and Music by Elton John,
Bernie Taupin and Davey Johnstone

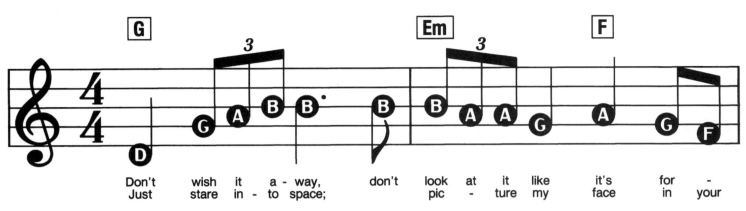

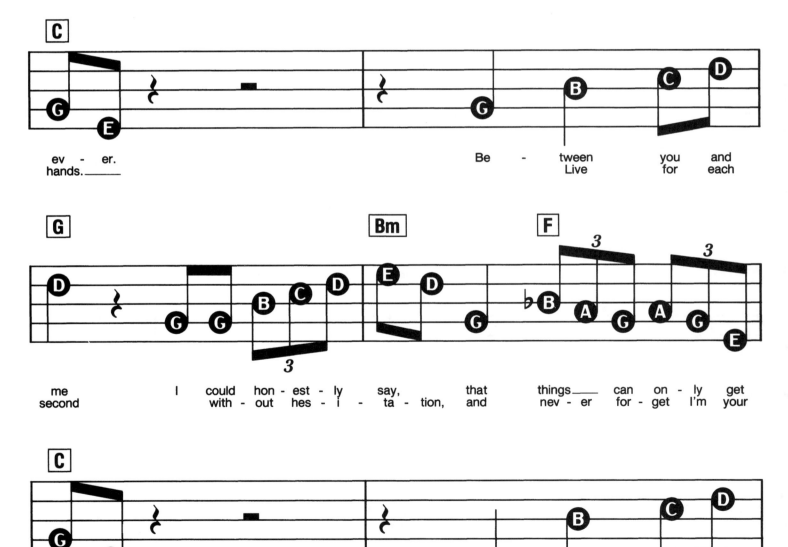

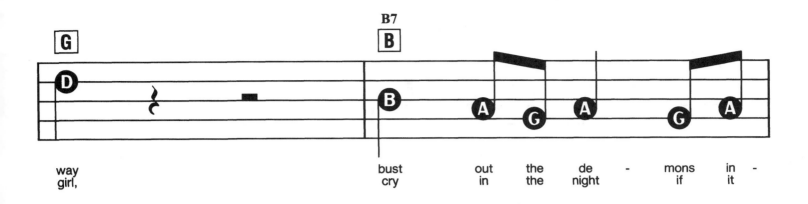

way
girl,

bust
cry

out
in

the
the

de -
night

mons
if

in -
it

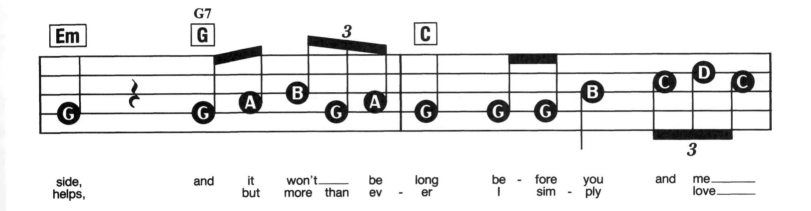

side,
helps,

and
but

it
more

won't____
than

be
ev -

long
er

be - fore
I

you
sim -

and
ply

me____
love____

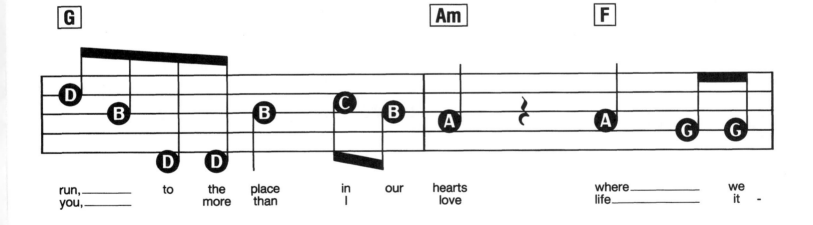

run,____
you,____

to
the

the
more

place
than

in
I

our
love

hearts

where____
life____

we
it -

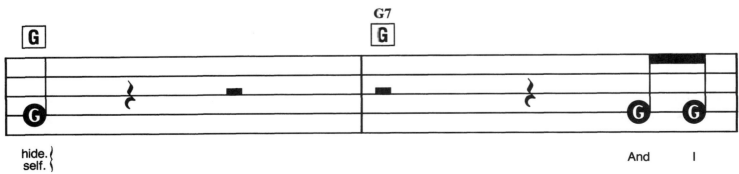

hide.
self.

And

I

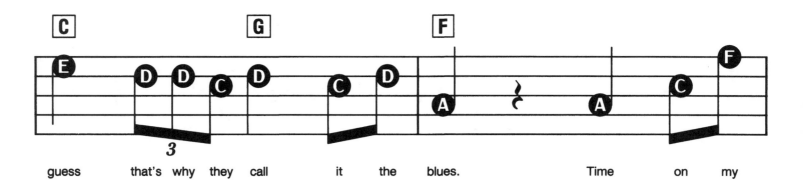

guess that's why they call it the blues. Time on my

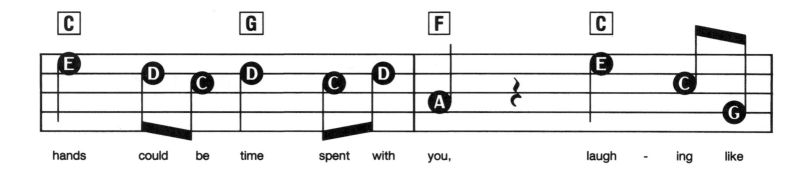

hands could be time spent with you, laugh - ing like

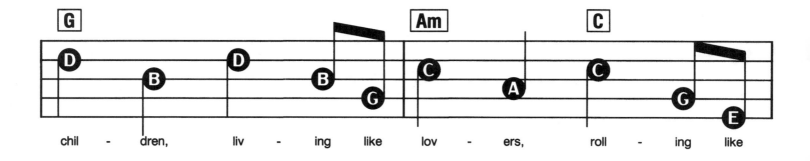

chil - dren, liv - ing like lov - ers, roll - ing like

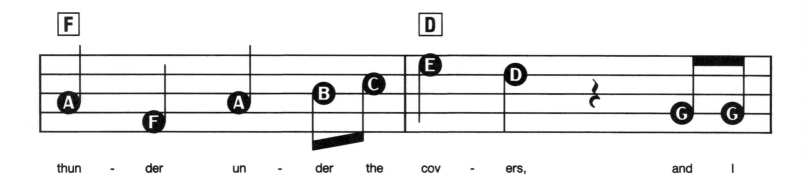

thun - der un - der the cov - ers, and I

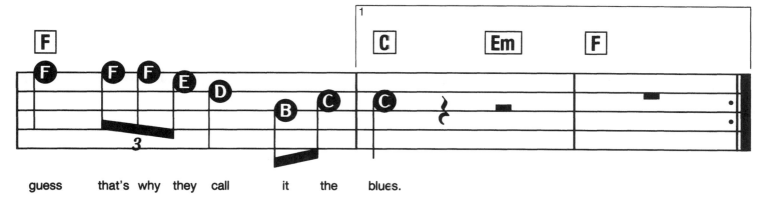

guess that's why they call it the blues.

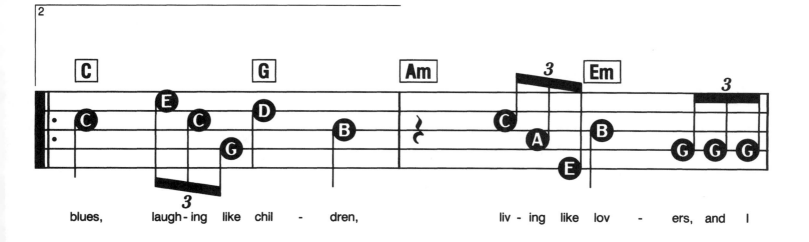

blues, laugh-ing like chil - dren, liv - ing like lov - ers, and I

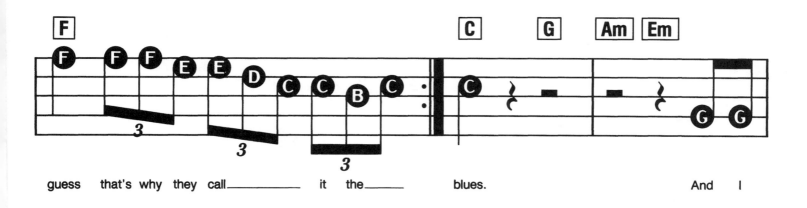

guess that's why they call_____ it the_____ blues. And I

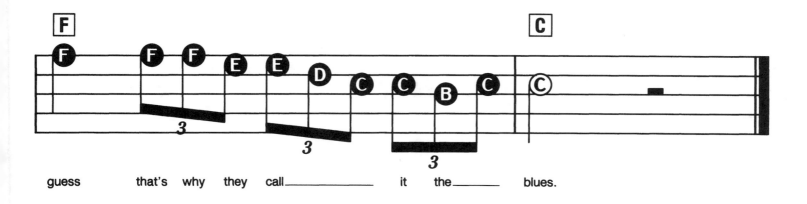

guess that's why they call_____ it the_____ blues.

I Want Love

Registration 8
Rhythm: 8-Beat or Rock

Words and Music by Elton John
and Bernie Taupin

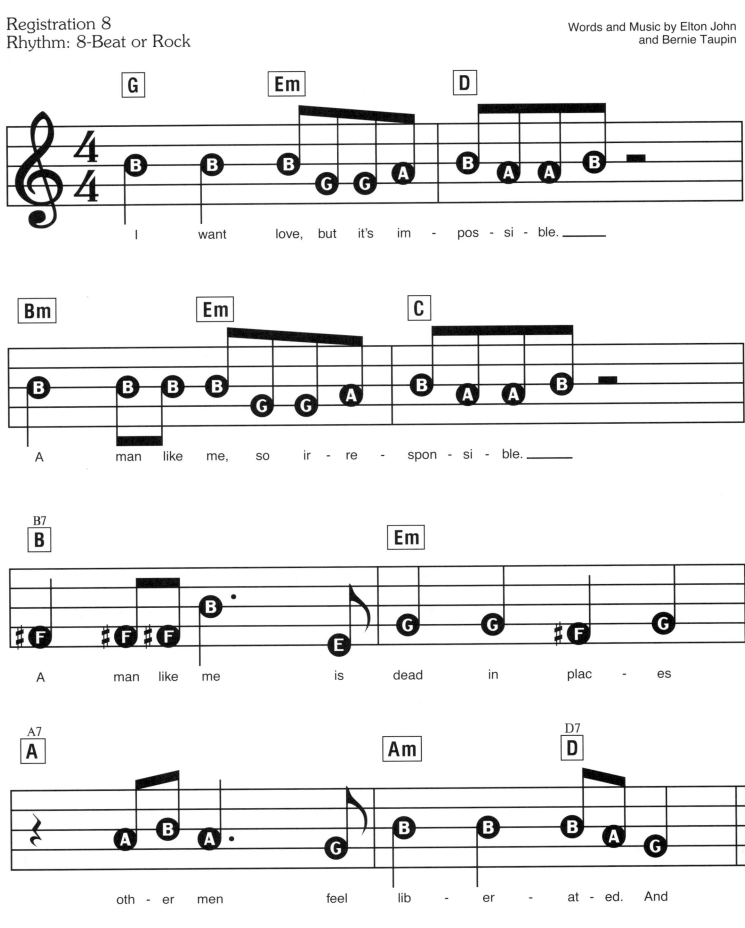

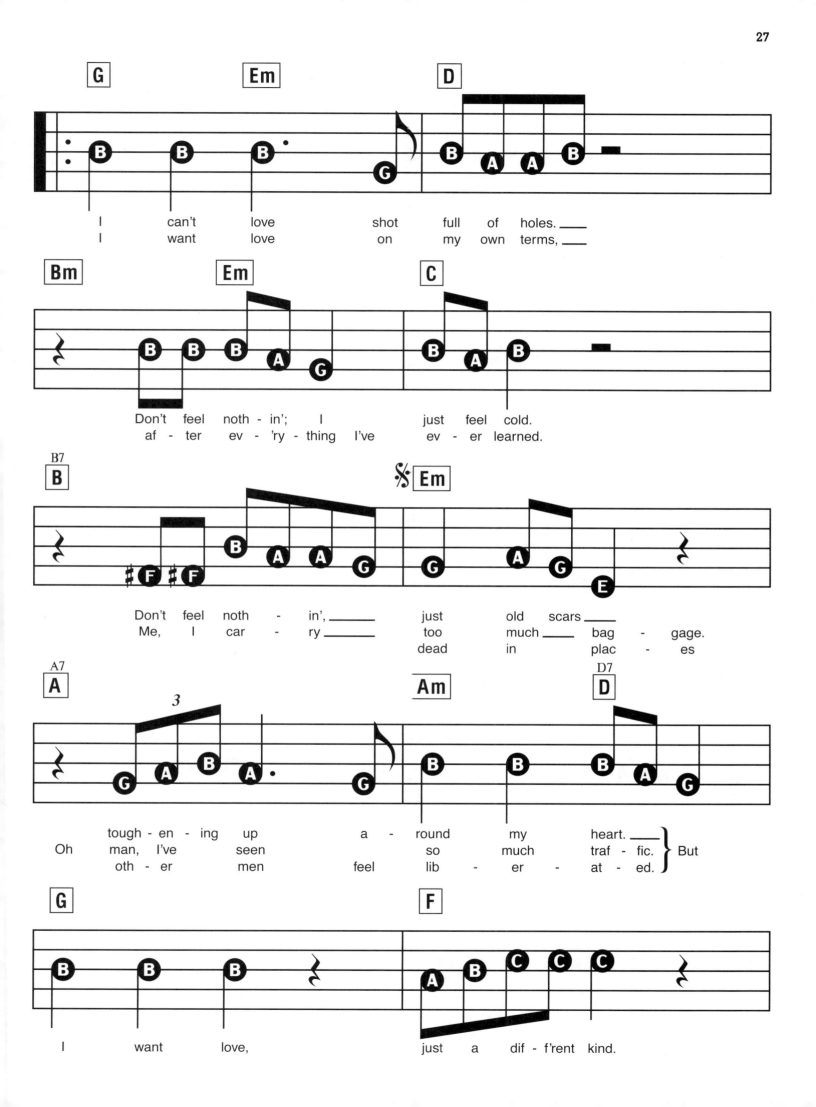

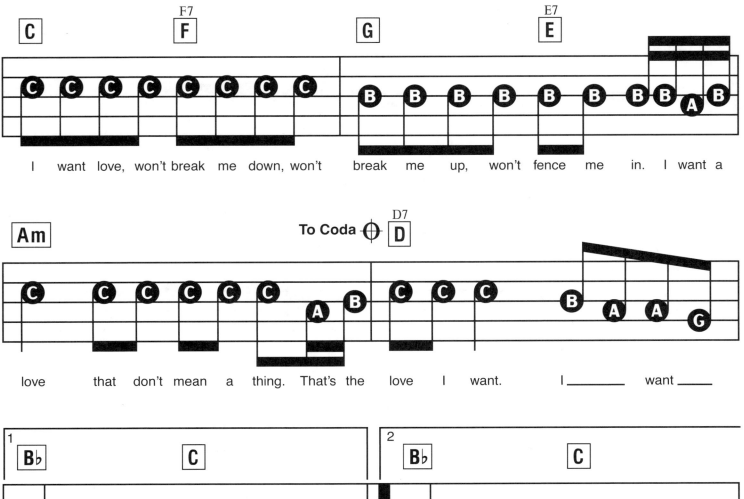

I want love, won't break me down, won't break me up, won't fence me in. I want a

love that don't mean a thing. That's the love I want. I _____ want _____

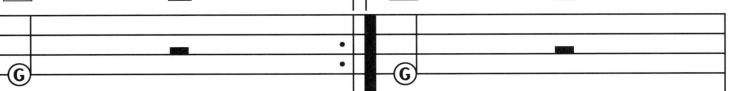

love.   love.

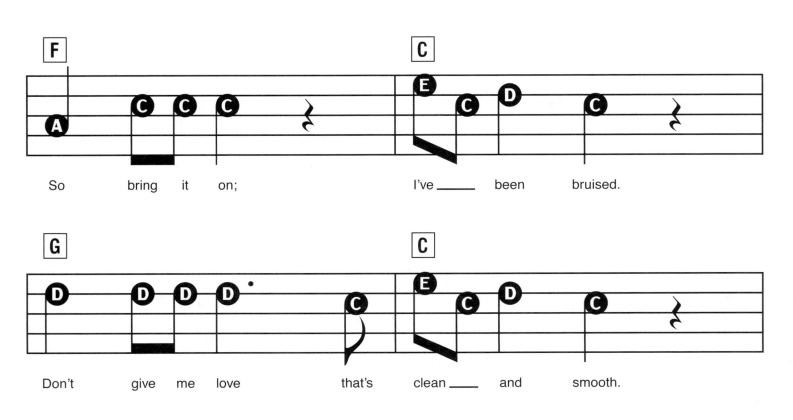

So   bring   it   on;   I've ____ been   bruised.

Don't   give   me   love   that's   clean ____ and   smooth.

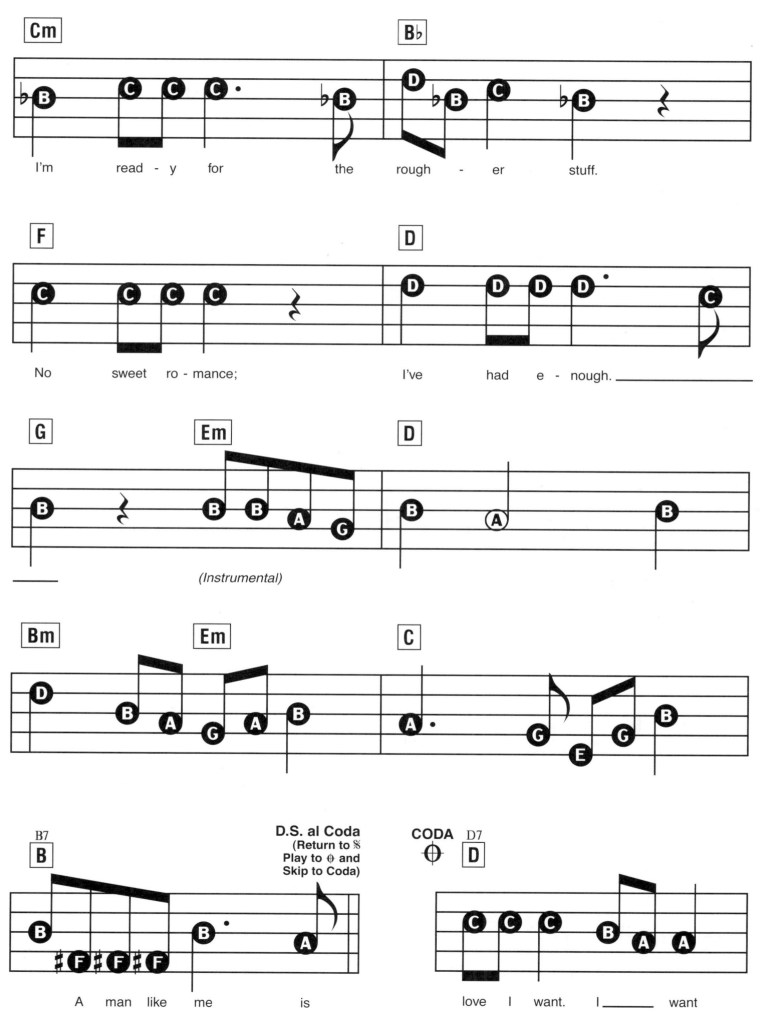

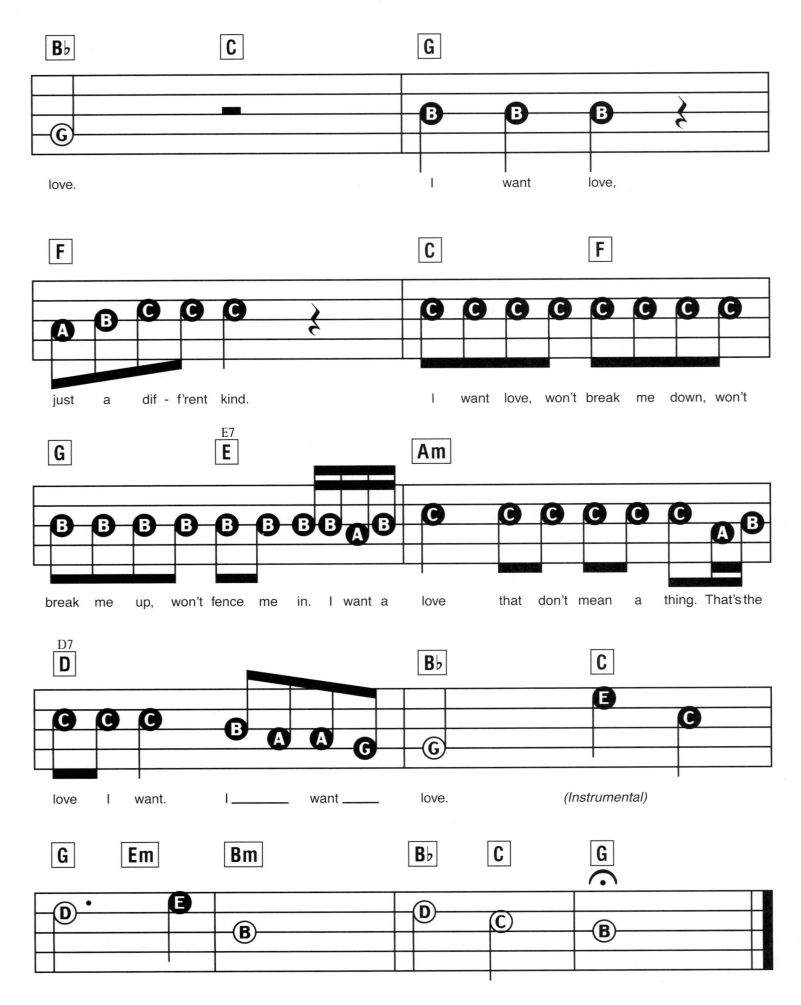

Made for Me

Registration 8
Rhythm: 8-Beat or Rock

Words and Music by Elton John
and Bernie Taupin

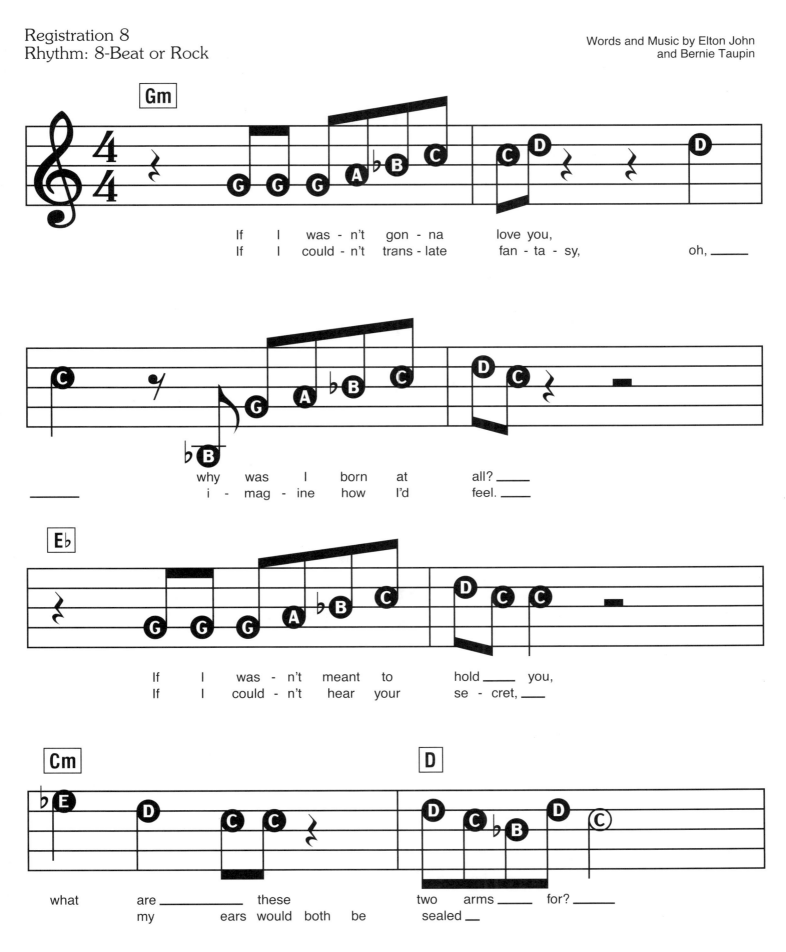

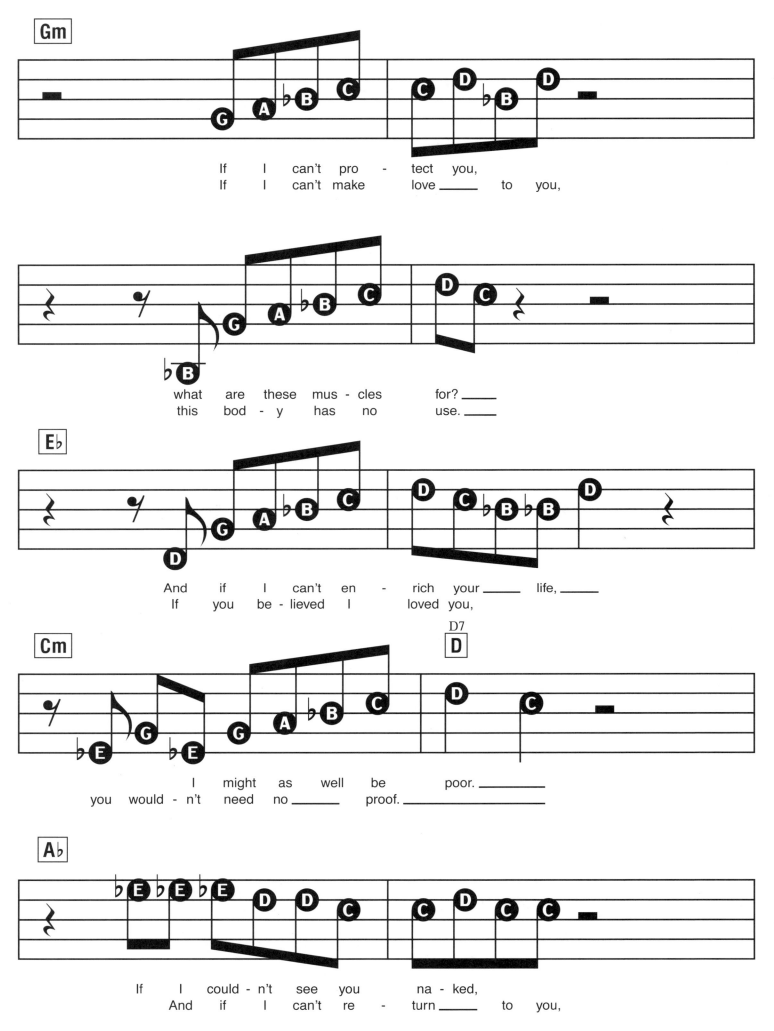

33

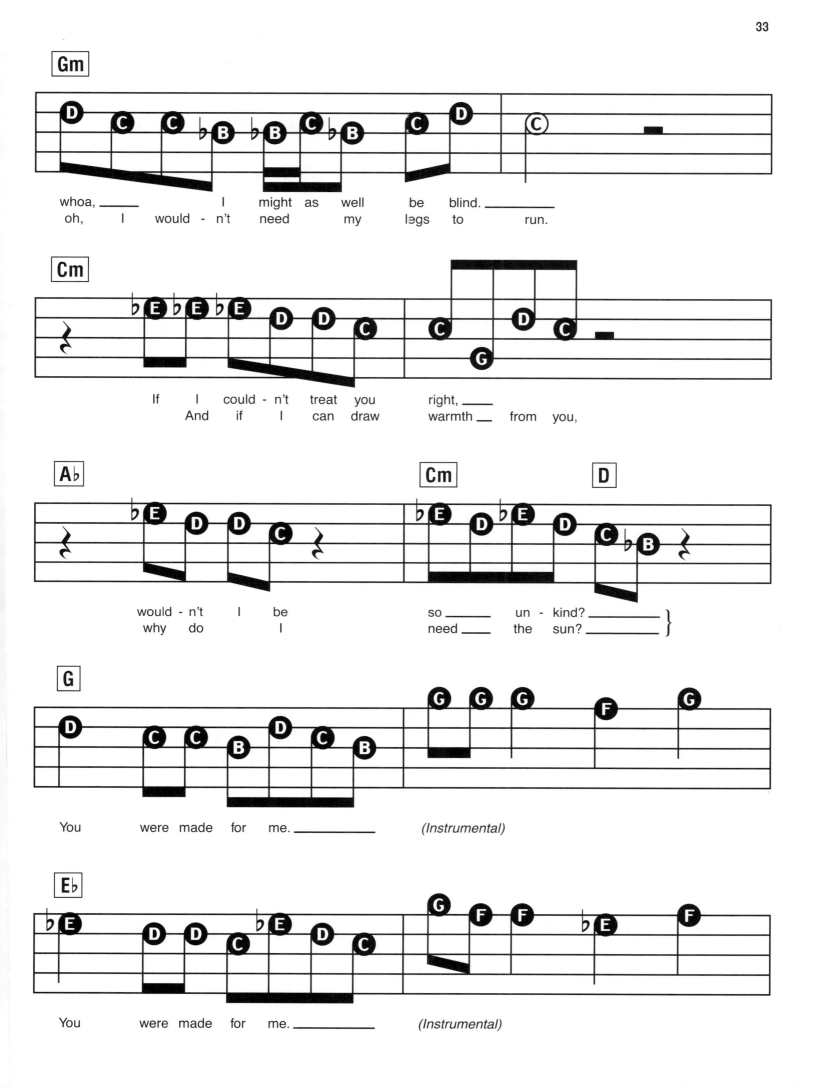

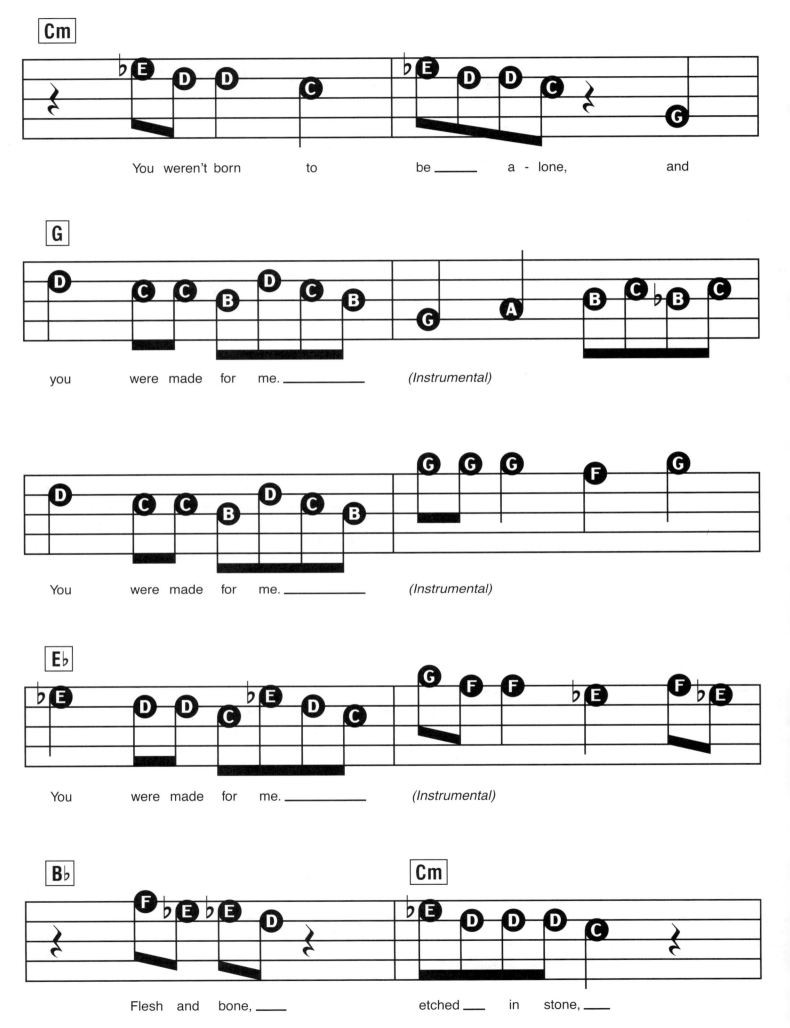

Cm

You weren't born to be _____ a - lone, and

G

you were made for me. _____ *(Instrumental)*

You were made for me. _____ *(Instrumental)*

E♭

You were made for me. _____ *(Instrumental)*

B♭

Flesh and bone, _____

Cm

etched _____ in stone, _____

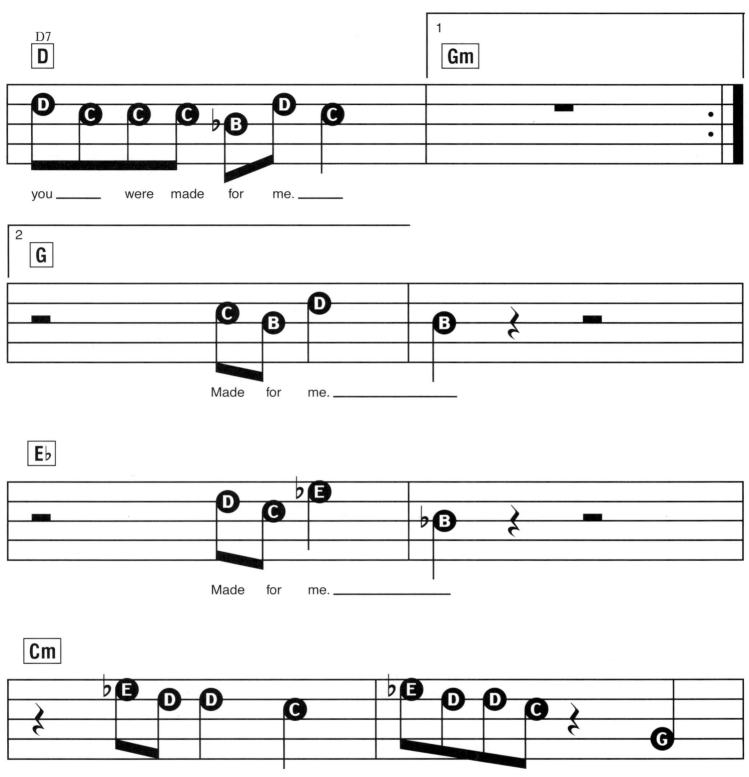

you _____ were made for me. _____

Made for me. _____

Made for me. _____

You weren't born to be _____ a - lone, and

you were made for me. _____ *(Instrumental)*

I've Been Loving You

Registration 8
Rhythm: 8-Beat or Rock

Words and Music by Elton John
and Bernie Taupin

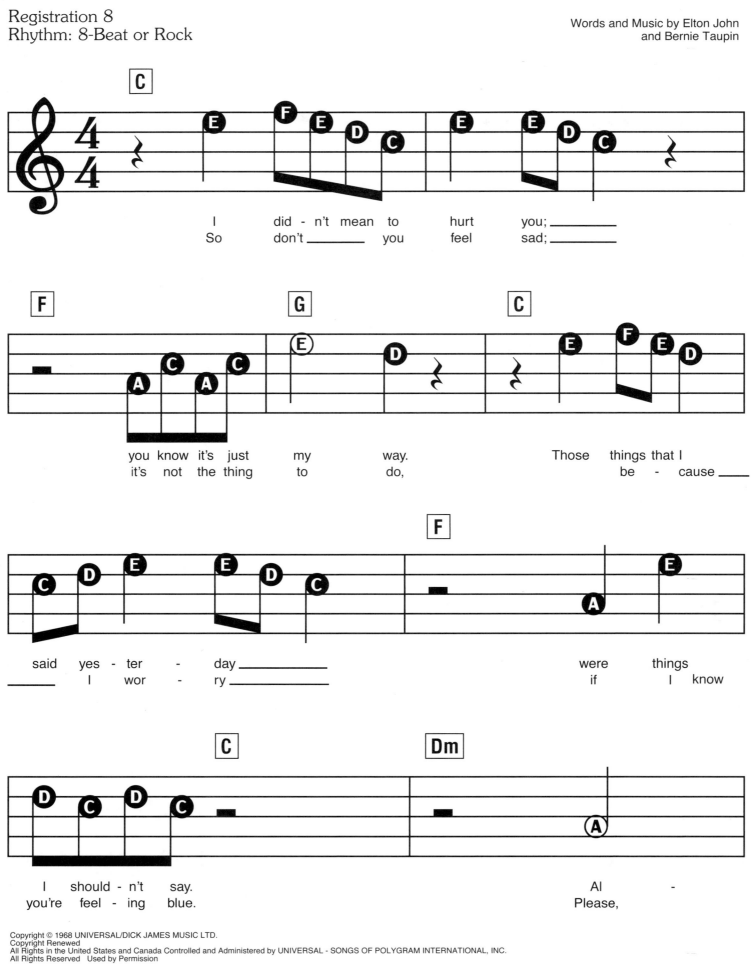

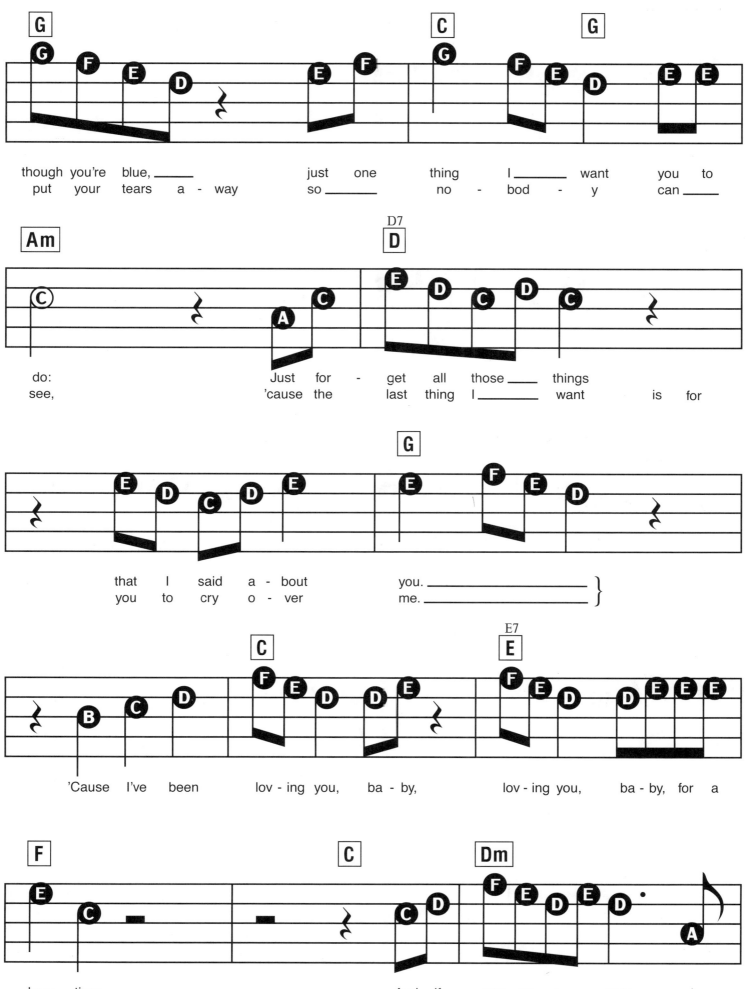

38

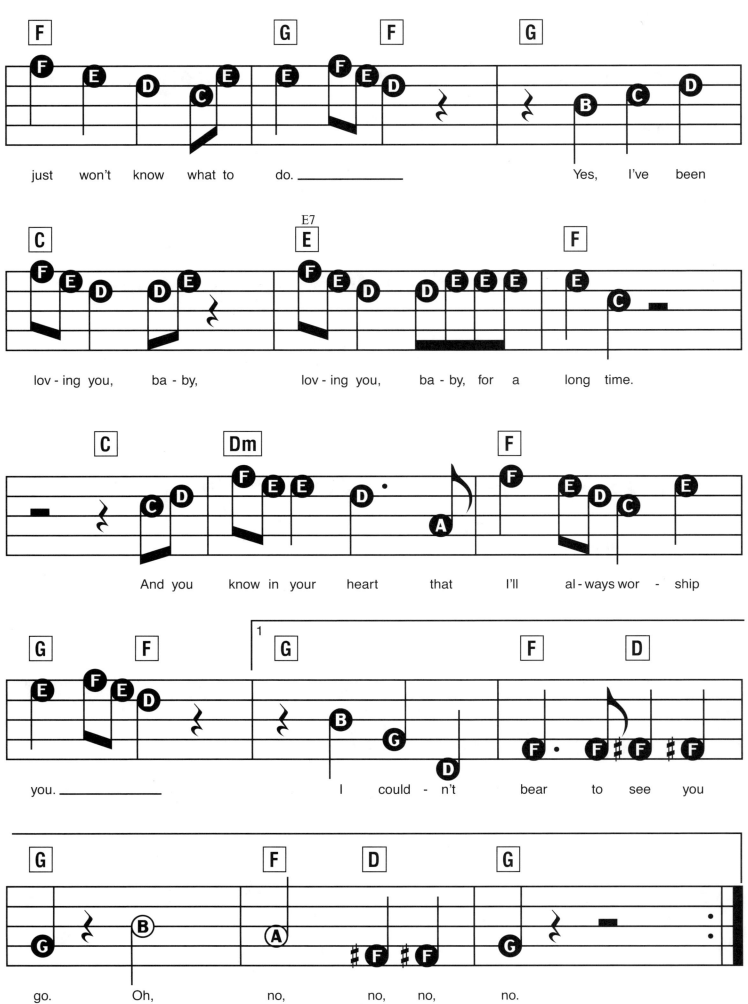

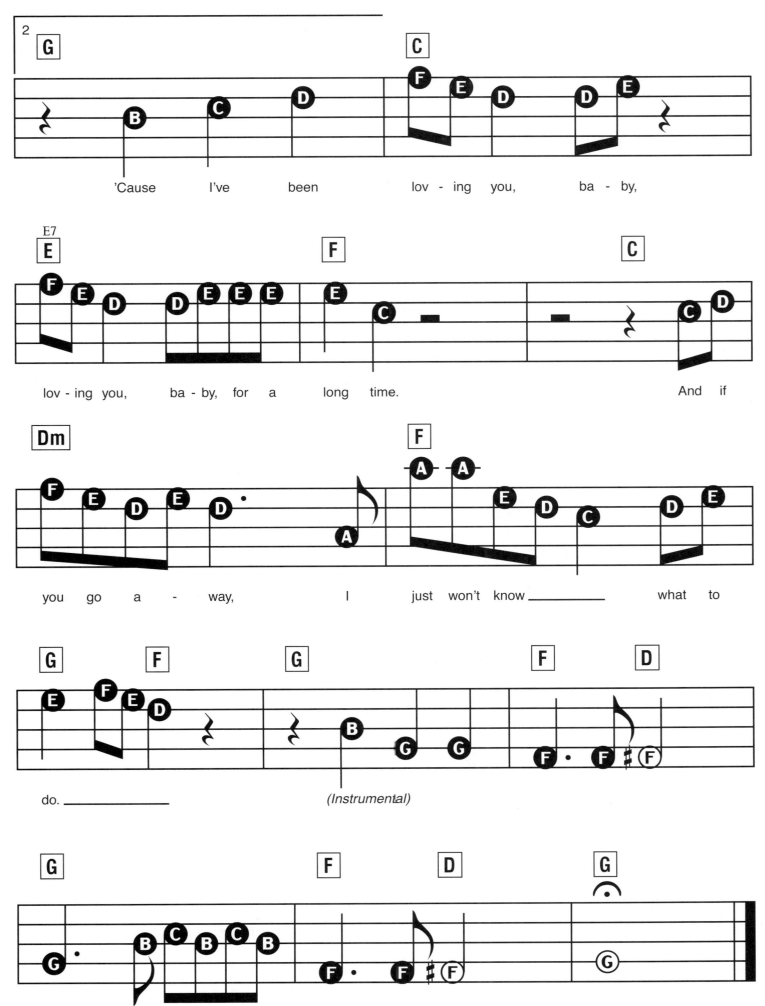

Little Jeannie

Registration 4
Rhythm: Latin or Bossa Nova

Words and Music by Elton John
and Gary Osborne

41

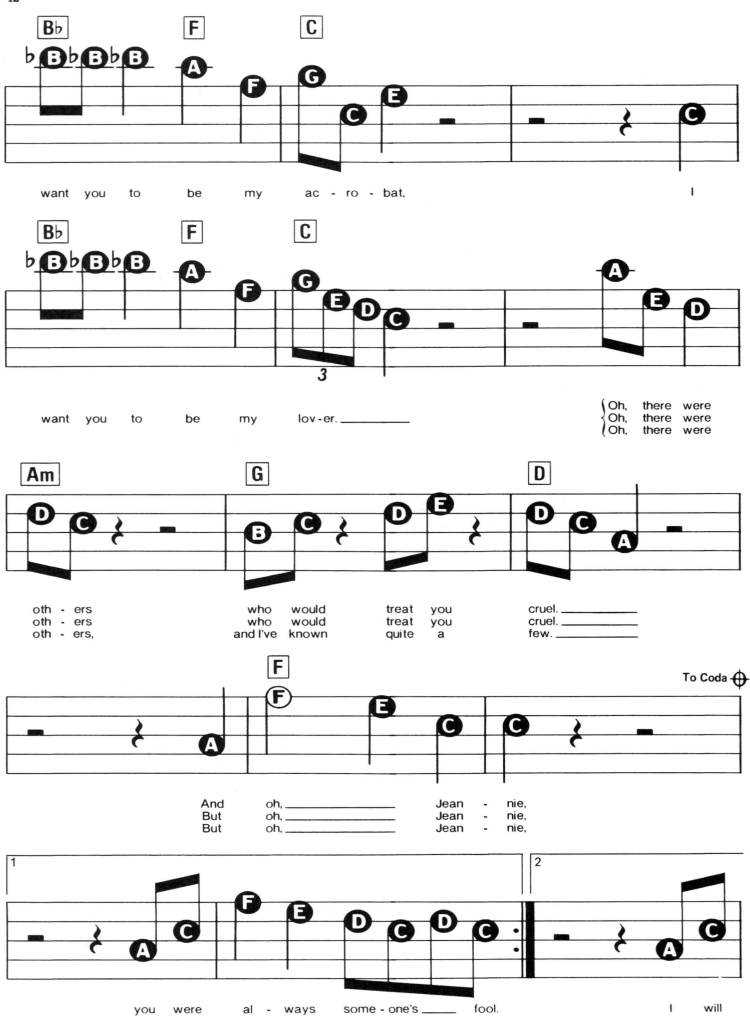

42

D.S. al Coda
(Return to %
Play to ⊕ and
skip to Coda)

⊕ CODA

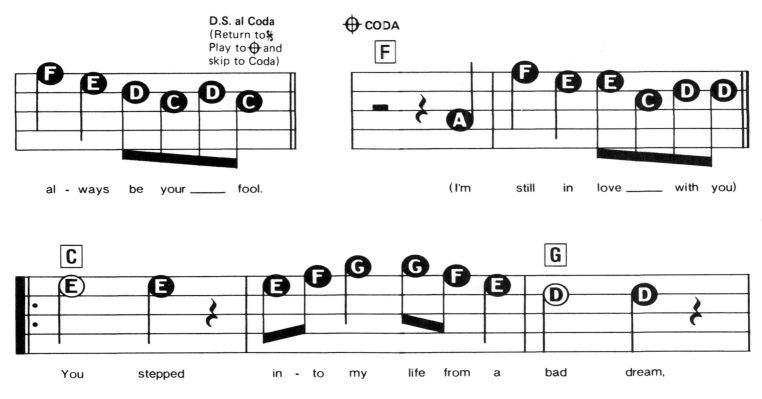

al - ways be your ____ fool.

(I'm still in love ____ with you)

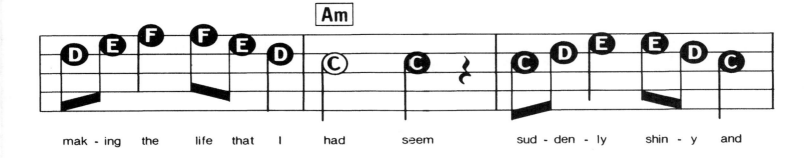

You stepped in - to my life from a bad dream,

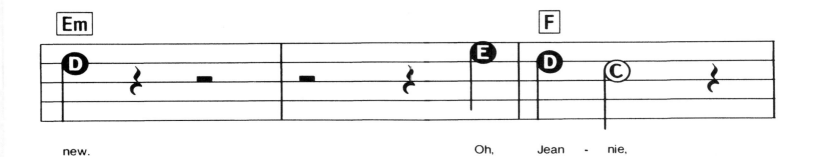

mak - ing the life that I had seem sud - den - ly shin - y and

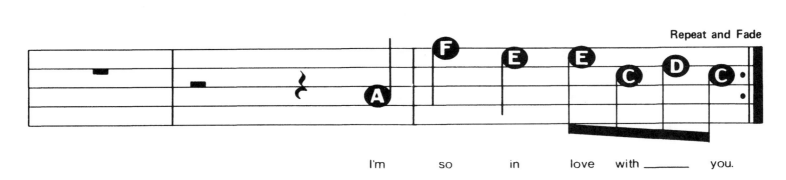

new.   Oh, Jean - nie,

Repeat and Fade

I'm so in love with ____ you.

Michelle's Song
from the Motion Picture FRIENDS

Registration 7
Rhythm: Rock

Words and Music by Elton John
and Bernie Taupin

Cast a peb - ble on the wa - ter, watch the
Sleep - ing in the o - pen, see the
learned to be so grace - ful, watch - ing

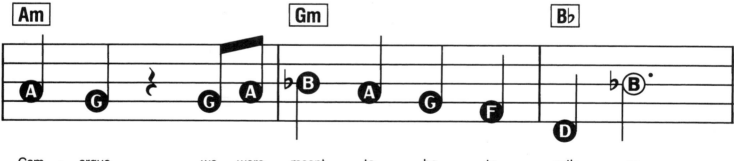

rip - ples gent - ly spread - ing, ti - ny daugh - ter of the
shad - ows soft - ly mov - ing, take a train to - wards the
wild_____ hors - es run - ning and_____ from those a - gile

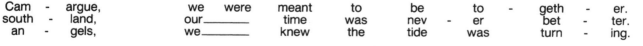

Cam - argue, we were meant to be to - geth - er.
south - land, our_____ time was nev - er bet - ter.
an - gels, we_____ knew the tide was turn - ing.

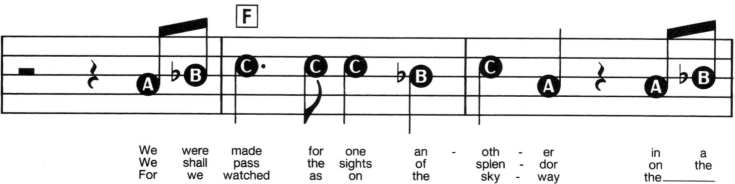

We were made for one an - oth - er in a
We shall pass for the sights of an - oth - er splen - dor on the
For we watched as on the sky - way the_____

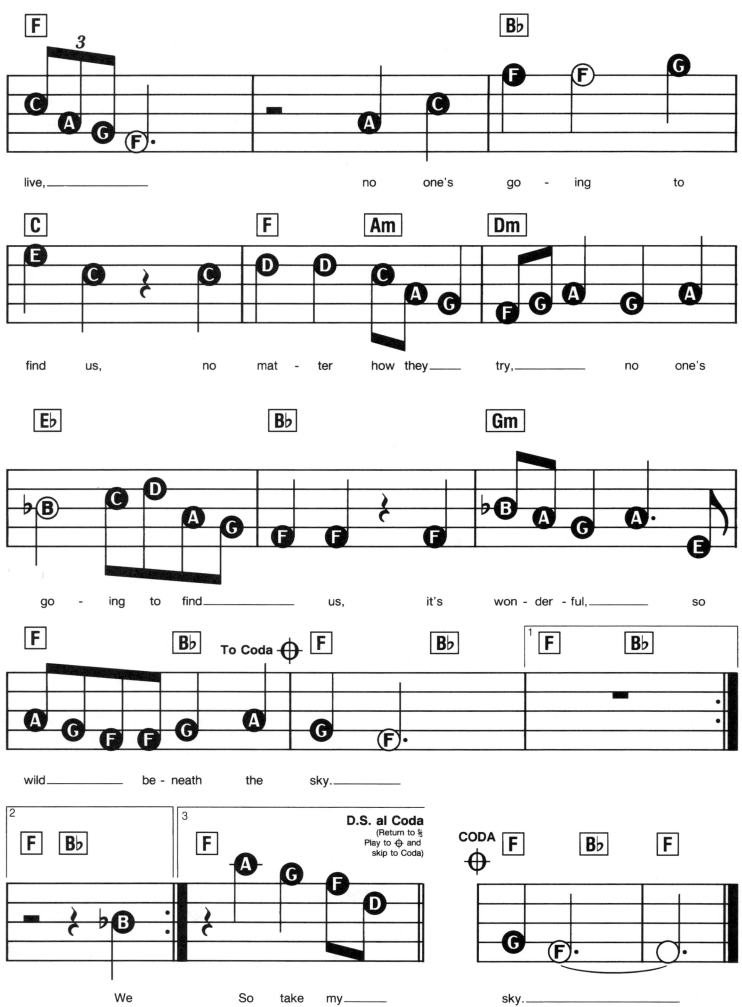

live,_____ no one's go - ing to

find us, no mat - ter how they_____ try,_____ no one's

go - ing to find_____ us, it's won - der - ful,_____ so

wild_____ be - neath the sky._____

We So take my_____

sky._____

Someday Out of the Blue
(Theme from El Dorado)
from THE ROAD TO EL DORADO

Registration 4
Rhythm: 8-Beat or Pop

Music by Elton John and Patrick Leonard
Lyrics by Tim Rice

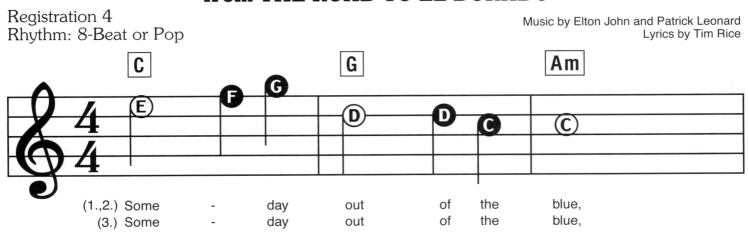

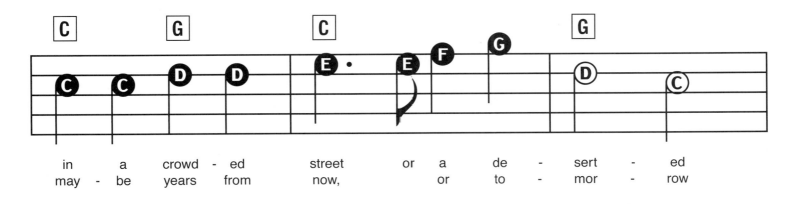

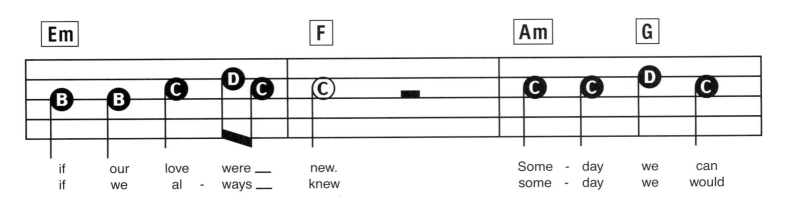

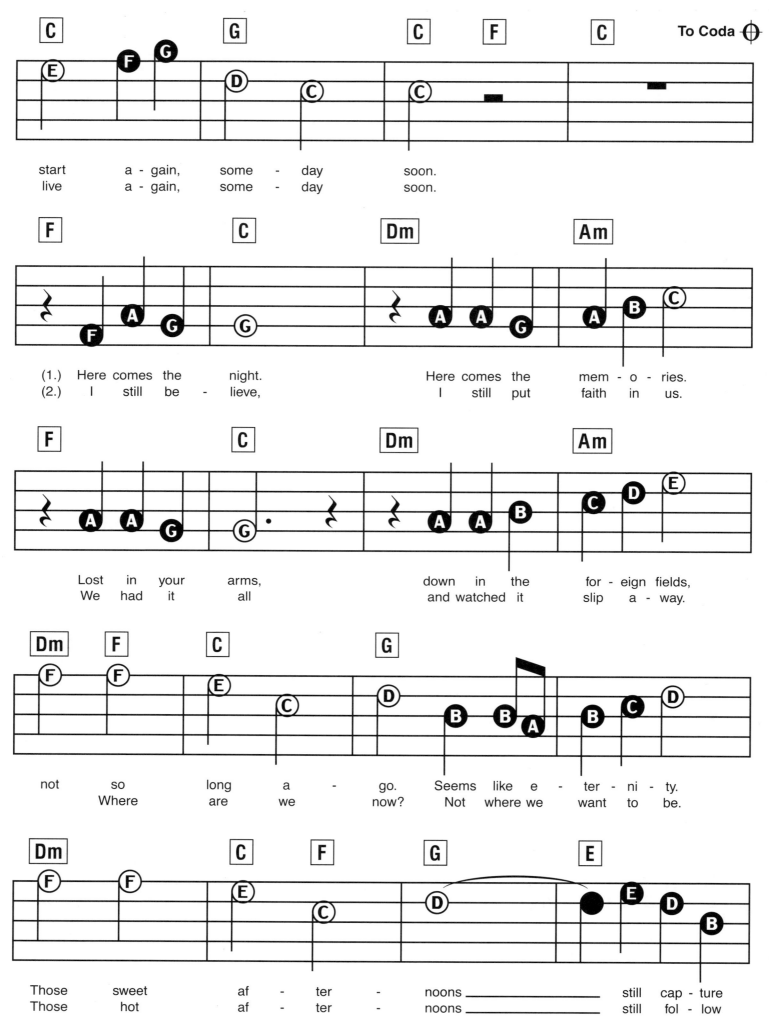

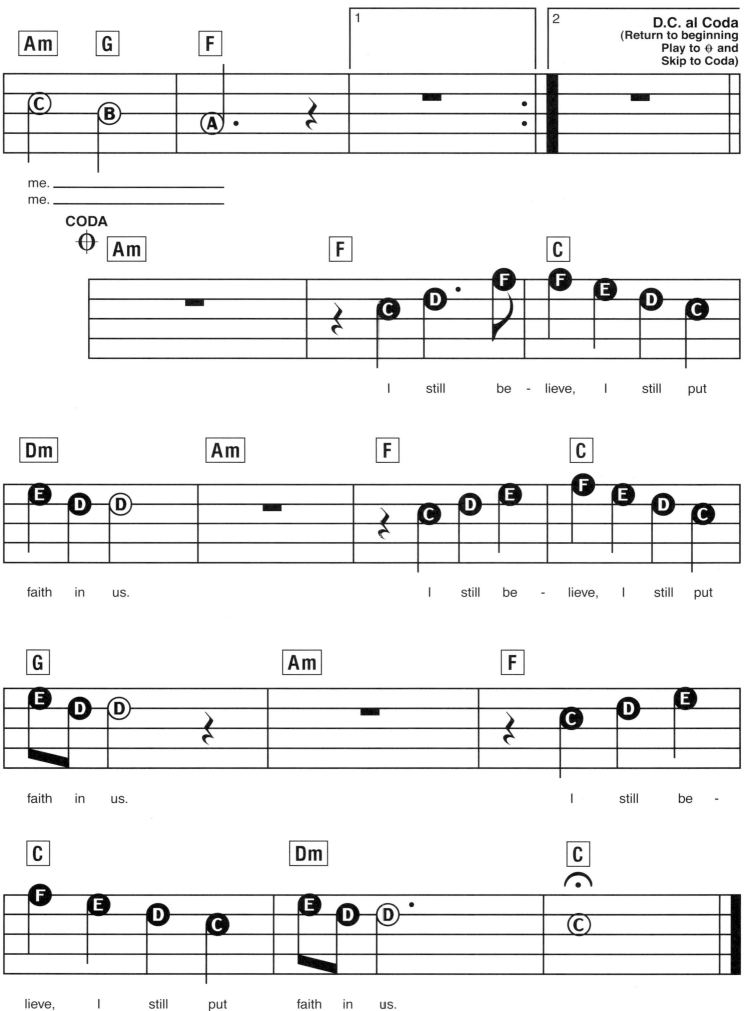

Nikita

Registration 4
Rhythm: Pops or 8-Beat

Words and Music by Elton John
and Bernie Taupin

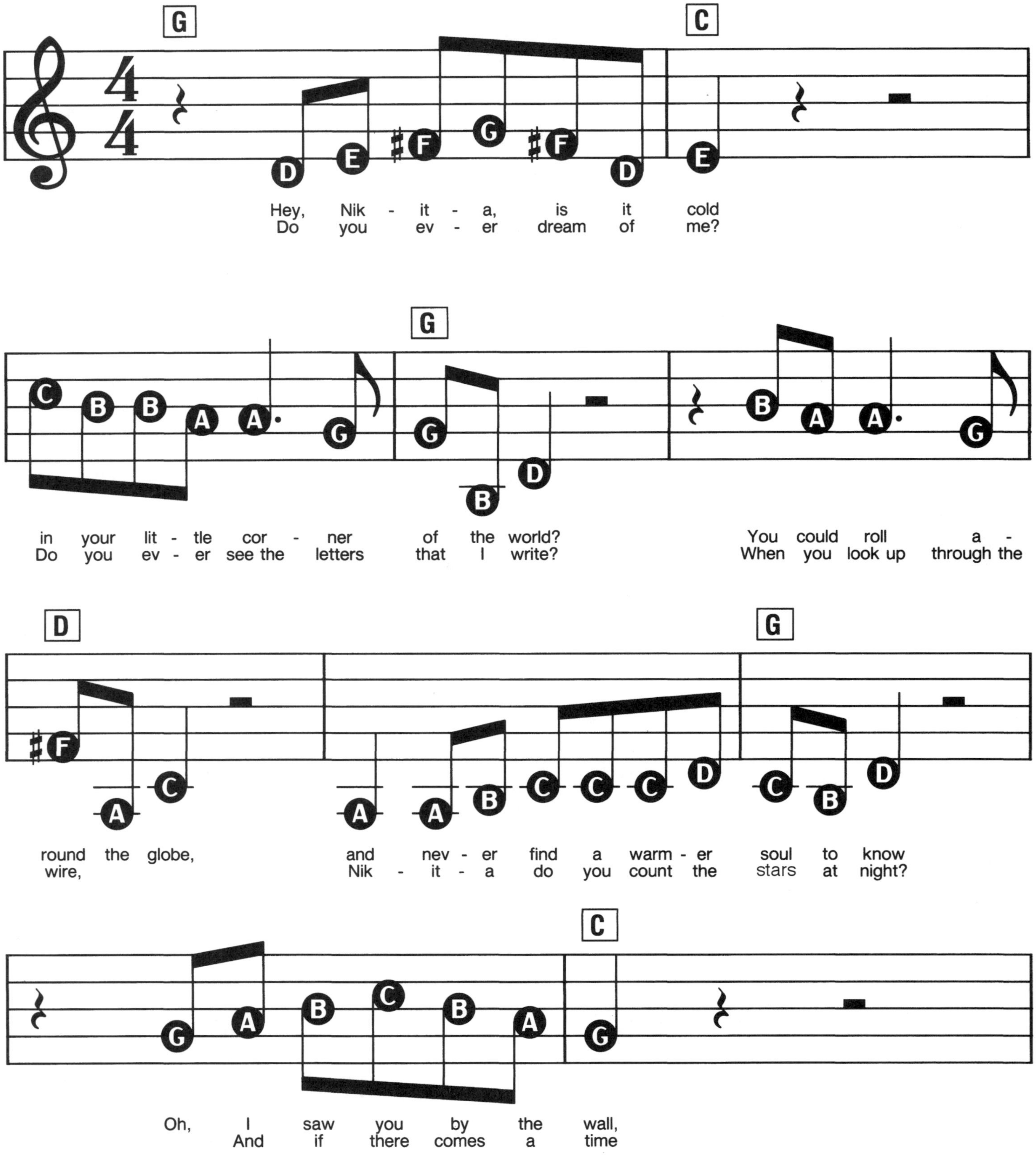

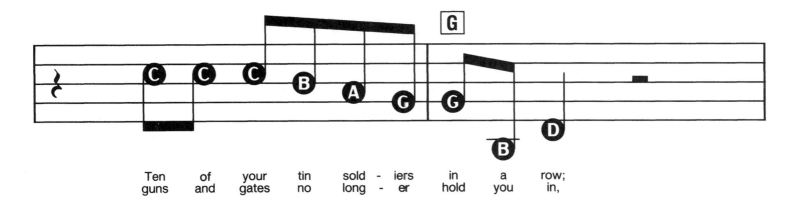

Ten of your tin sold - iers in a row;
guns and gates no long - er hold you in,

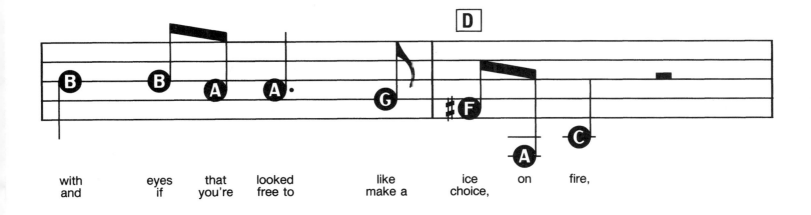

with eyes that looked like ice on fire,
and if you're free to make a choice,

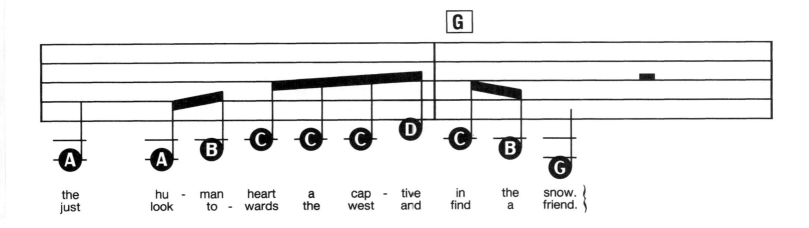

the hu - man heart a cap - tive in the snow.
just look to - wards the west and find a friend.

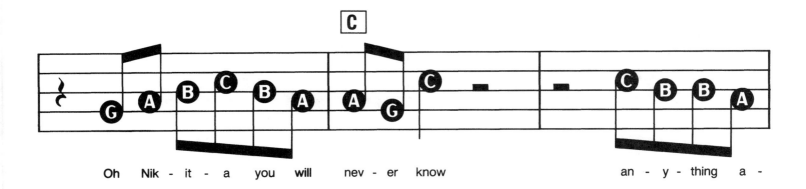

Oh Nik - it - a you will nev - er know an - y - thing a -

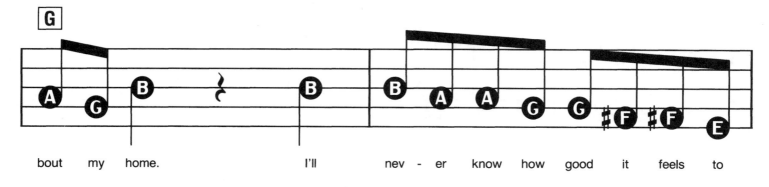

bout   my   home.   I'll   nev - er   know   how   good   it   feels   to

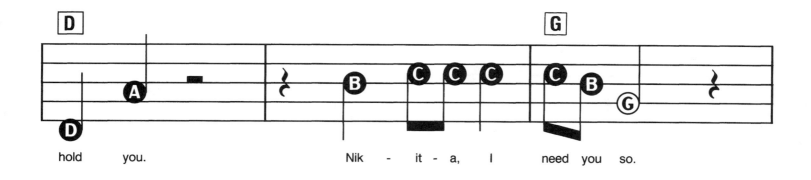

hold   you.   Nik - it - a,   I   need   you   so.

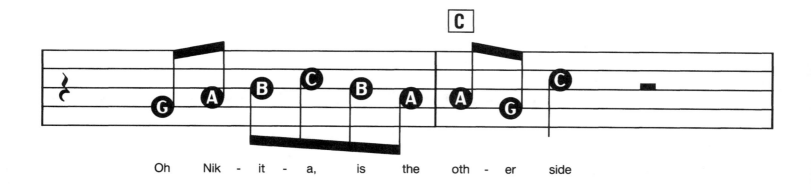

Oh   Nik - it - a,   is   the   oth - er   side

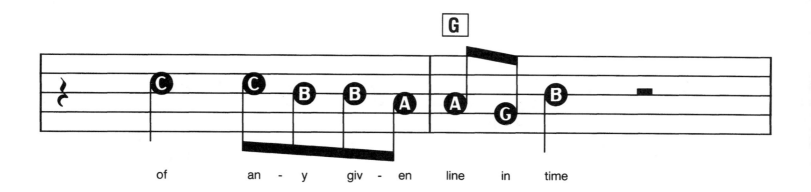

of   an - y   giv - en   line   in   time

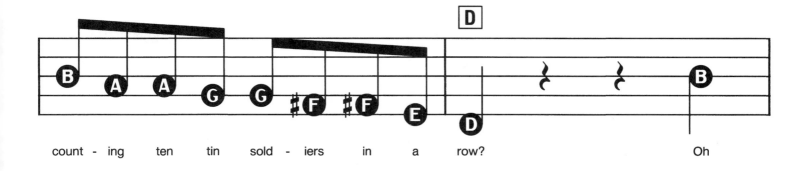

count - ing ten tin sold - iers in a row?   Oh

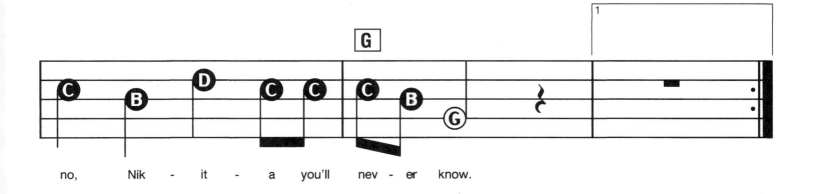

no,   Nik - it - a   you'll nev - er know.

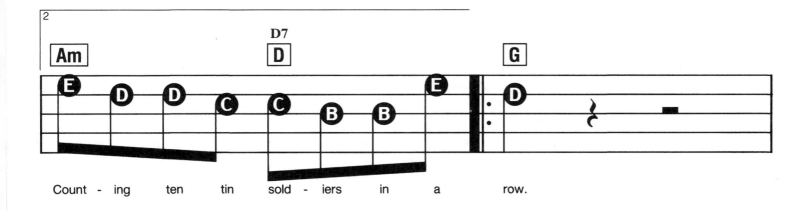

Count - ing   ten   tin   sold - iers   in   a   row.

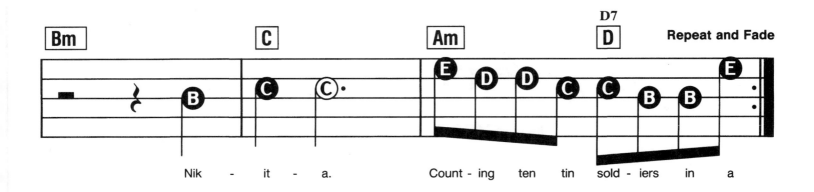

Nik - it - a.   Count - ing ten tin sold - iers in a

The One

Registration 8
Rhythm: Ballad or Pop

Words and Music by Elton John
and Bernie Taupin

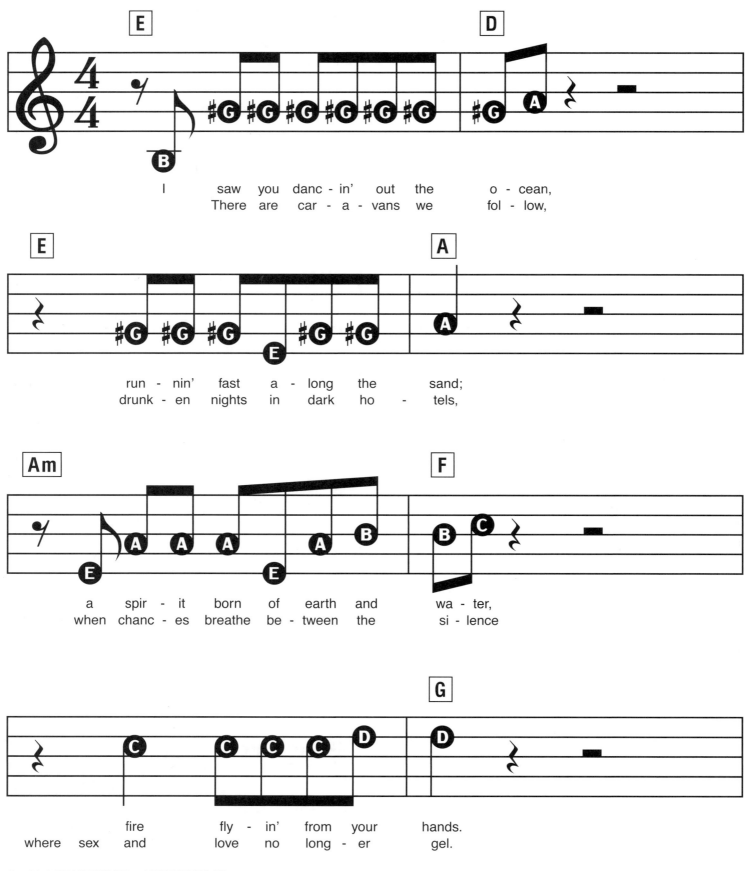

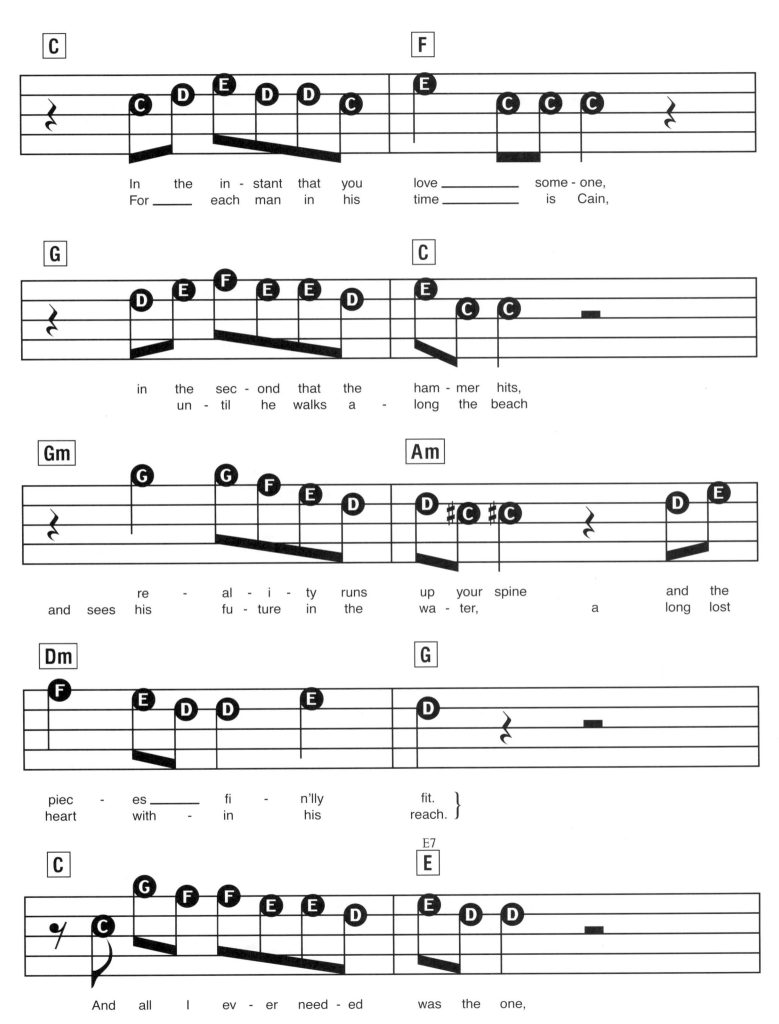

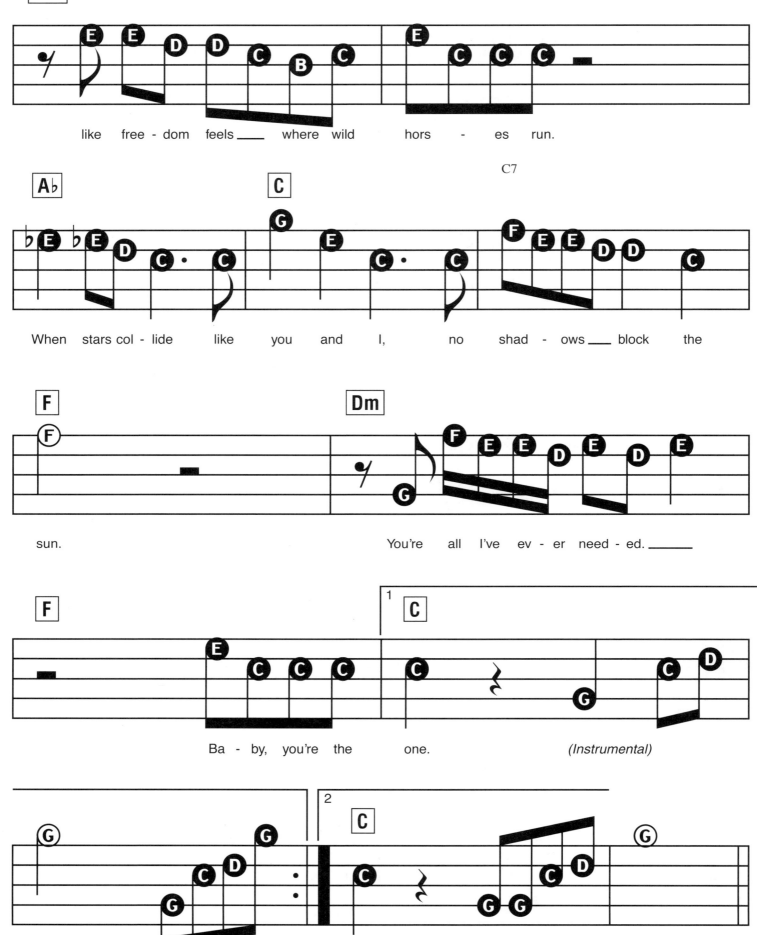

like free - dom feels ___ where wild hors - es run.

When stars col - lide like you and I, no shad - ows ___ block the

sun. You're all I've ev - er need - ed. _____

Ba - by, you're the one. *(Instrumental)*

one. *(Instrumental)*

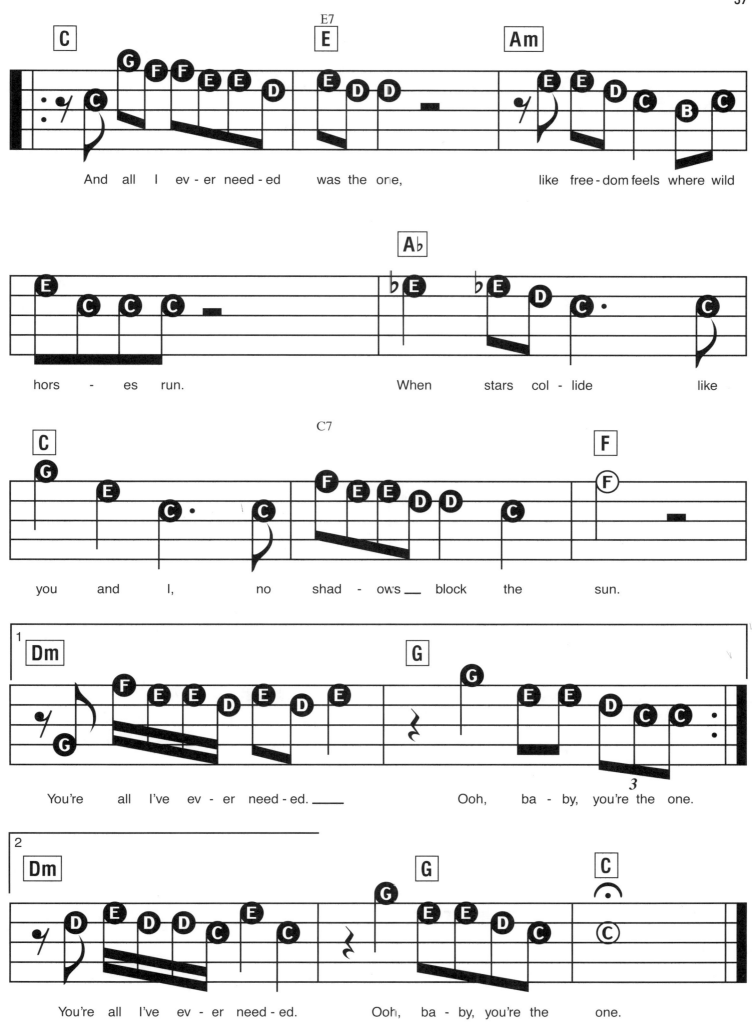

Something About the Way You Look Tonight

Registration 4
Rhythm: 8-Beat or Rock

Words and Music by Elton John
and Bernie Taupin

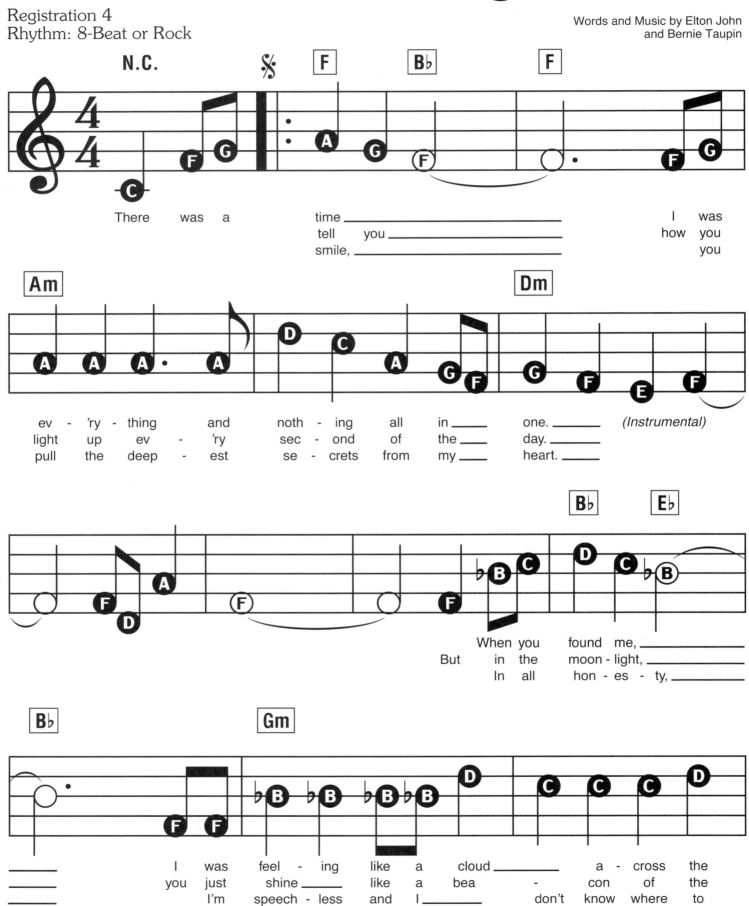

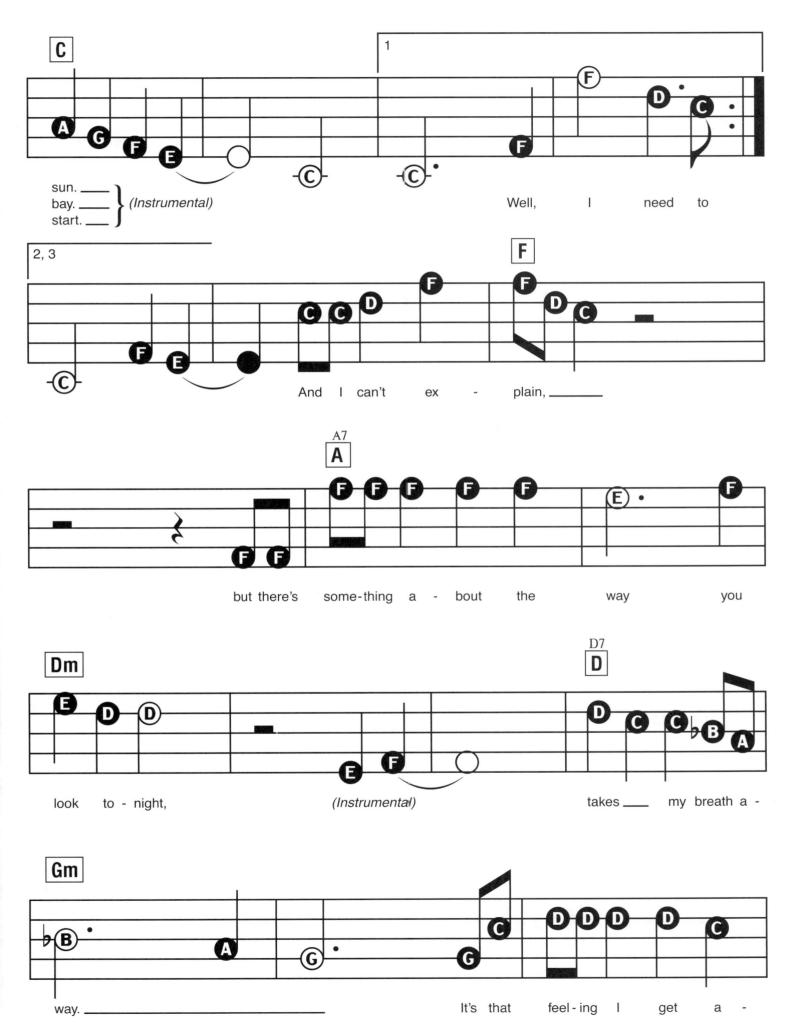

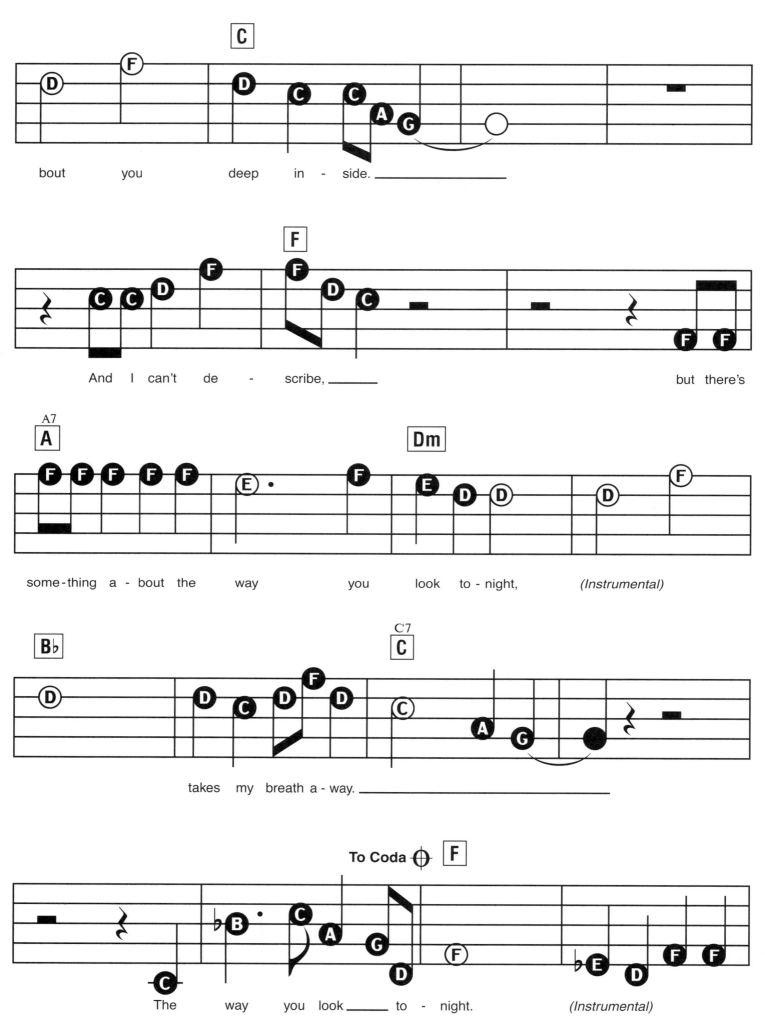

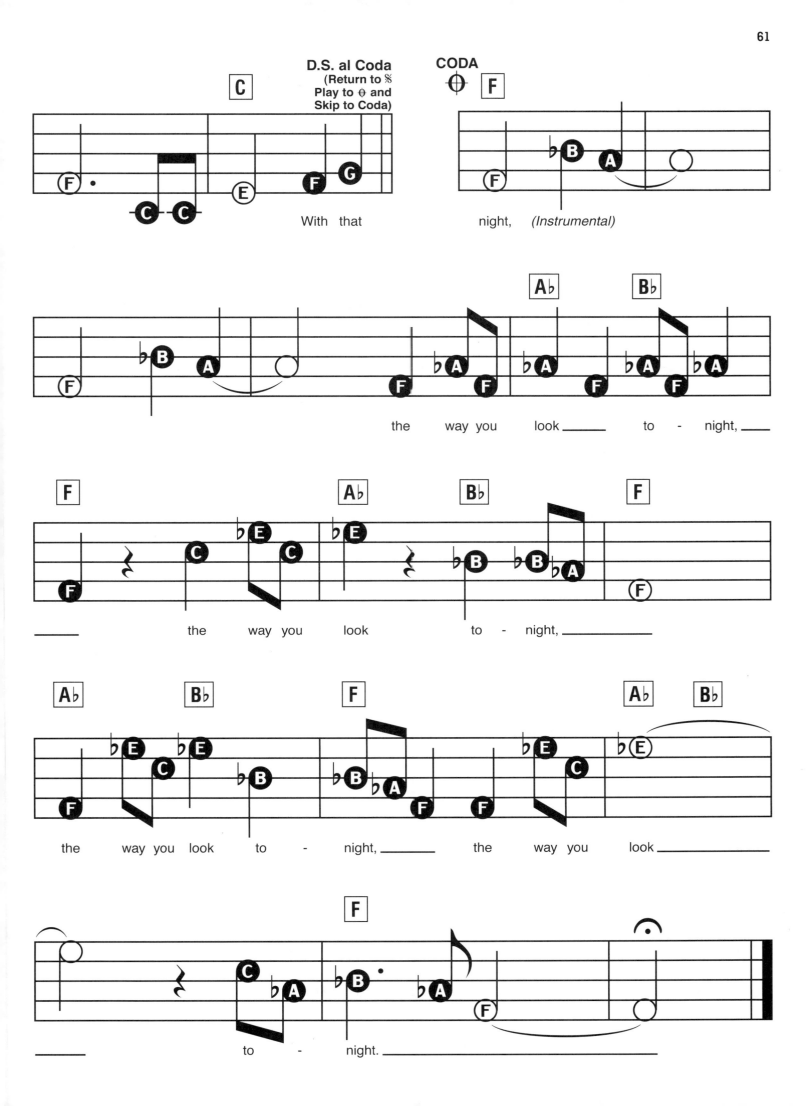

Sorry Seems to Be the Hardest Word

Registration 8
Rhythm: Ballad

Words and Music by Elton John
and Bernie Taupin

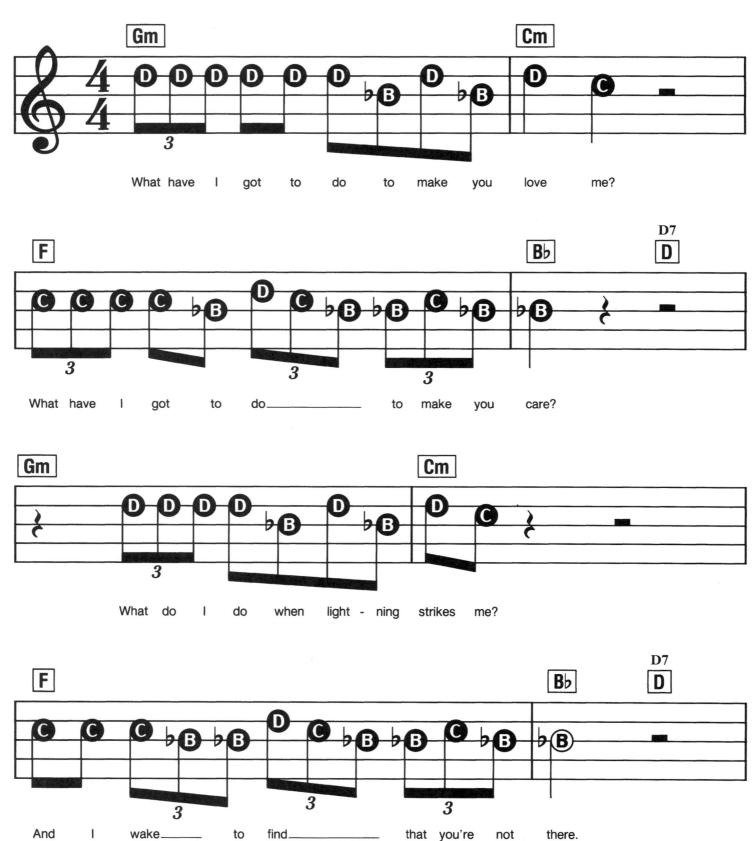

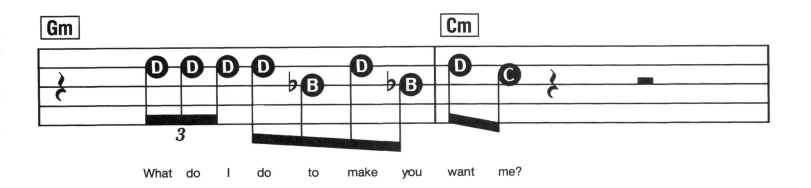

What do I do to make you want me?

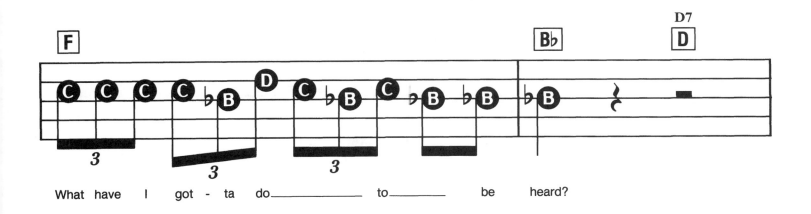

What have I got - ta do_____ to_____ be heard?

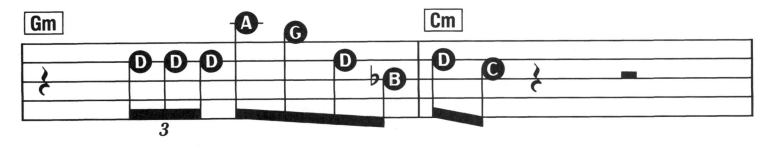

What do I say when it's all o - ver?

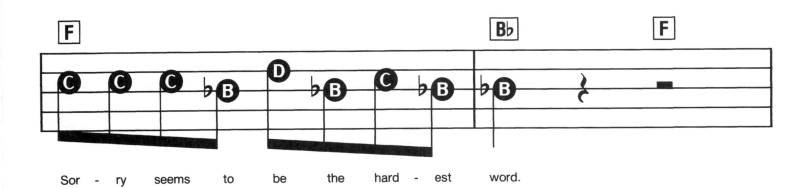

Sor - ry seems to be the hard - est word.

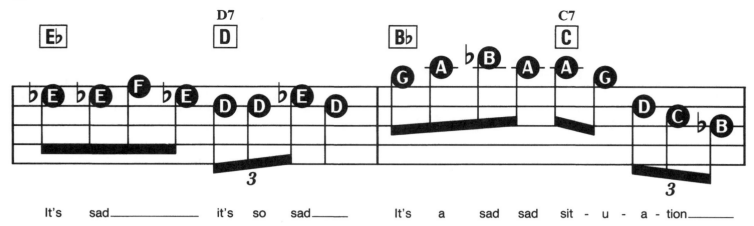

It's sad_____ it's so sad_____ It's a sad sad sit - u - a - tion_____

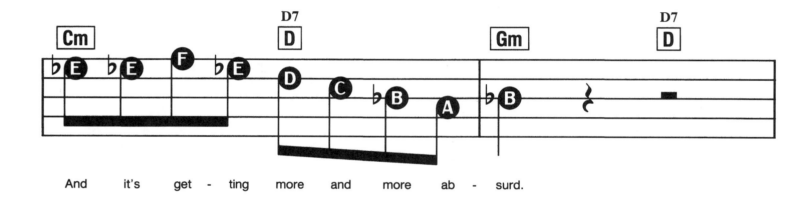

And it's get - ting more and more ab - surd.

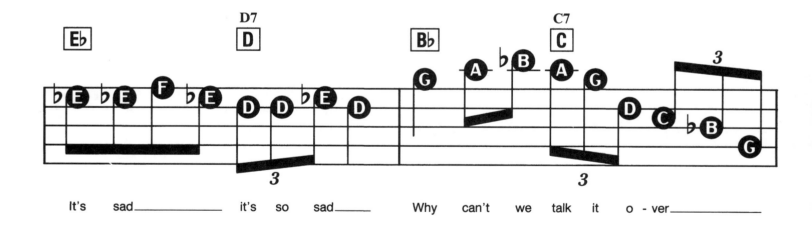

It's sad_____ it's so sad_____ Why can't we talk it o - ver_____

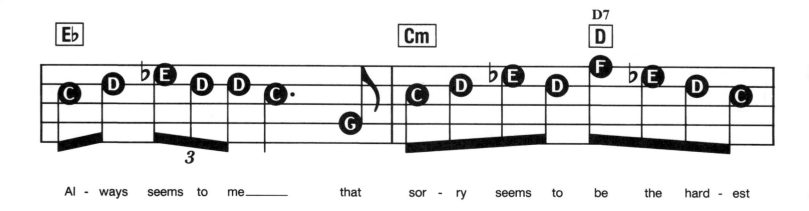

Al - ways seems to me_____ that sor - ry seems to be the hard - est

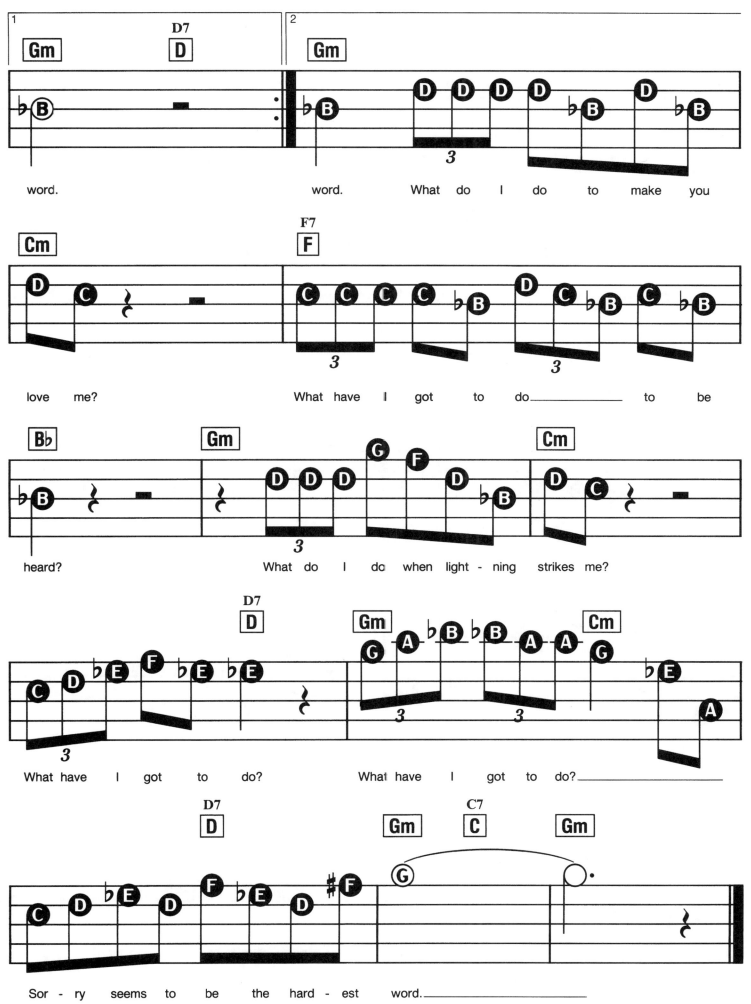

Written in the Stars
from Elton John and Tim Rice's AIDA

Registration 8
Rhythm: 8-Beat or Pops

Music by Elton John
Lyrics by Tim Rice

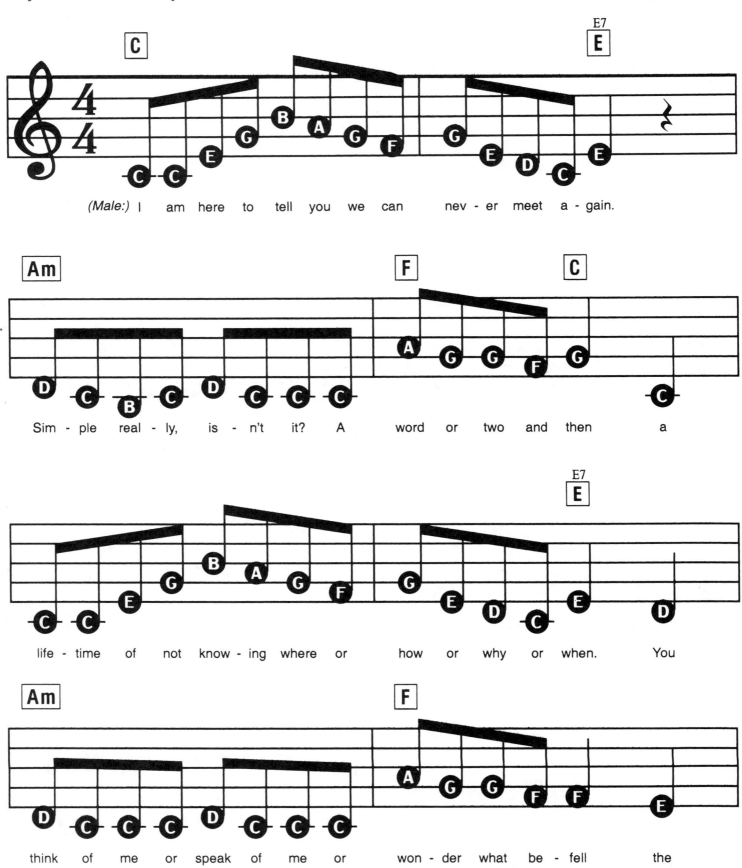

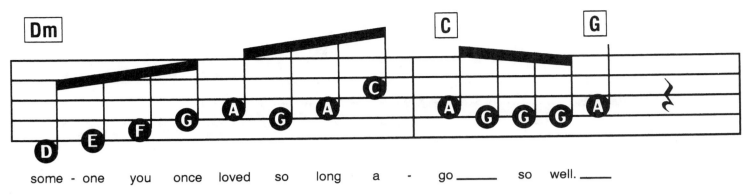

Dm · **C** · **G**

some - one you once loved so long a - go _____ so well. _____

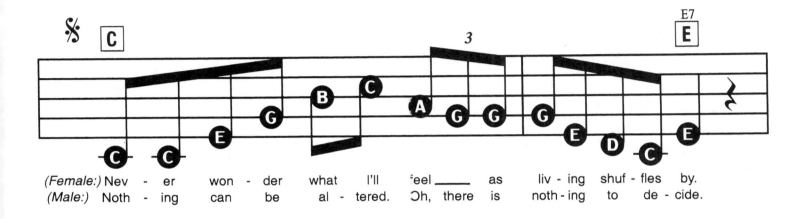

C · **E7** / **E**

(Female:) Nev - er won - der what I'll feel _____ as liv - ing shuf - fles by.
(Male:) Noth - ing can be al - tered. Oh, there is noth - ing to de - cide.

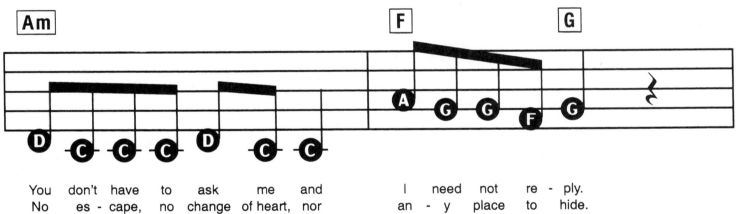

Am · **F** · **G**

You don't have to ask me and I need not re - ply.
No es - cape, no change of heart, nor an - y place to hide.

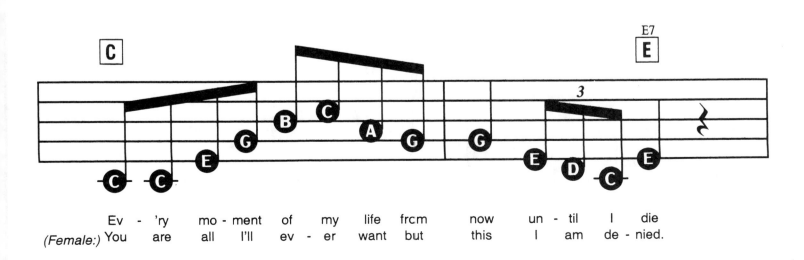

C · **E7** / **E**

Ev - 'ry mo - ment of my life from now un - til I die
(Female:) You are all I'll ev - er want but this I am de - nied.

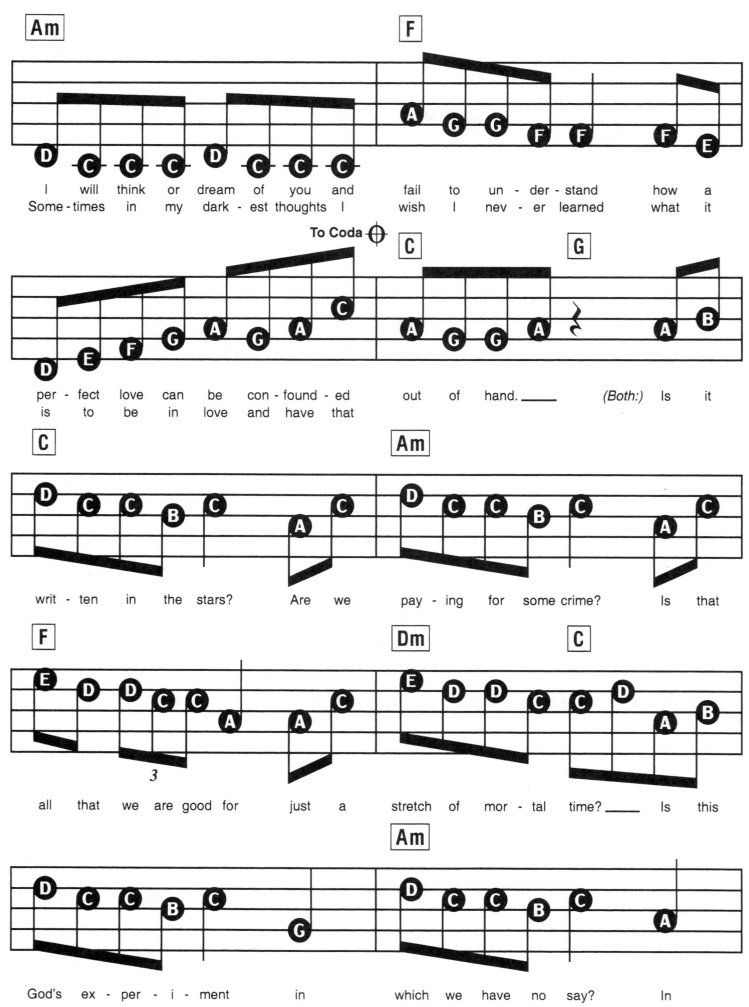

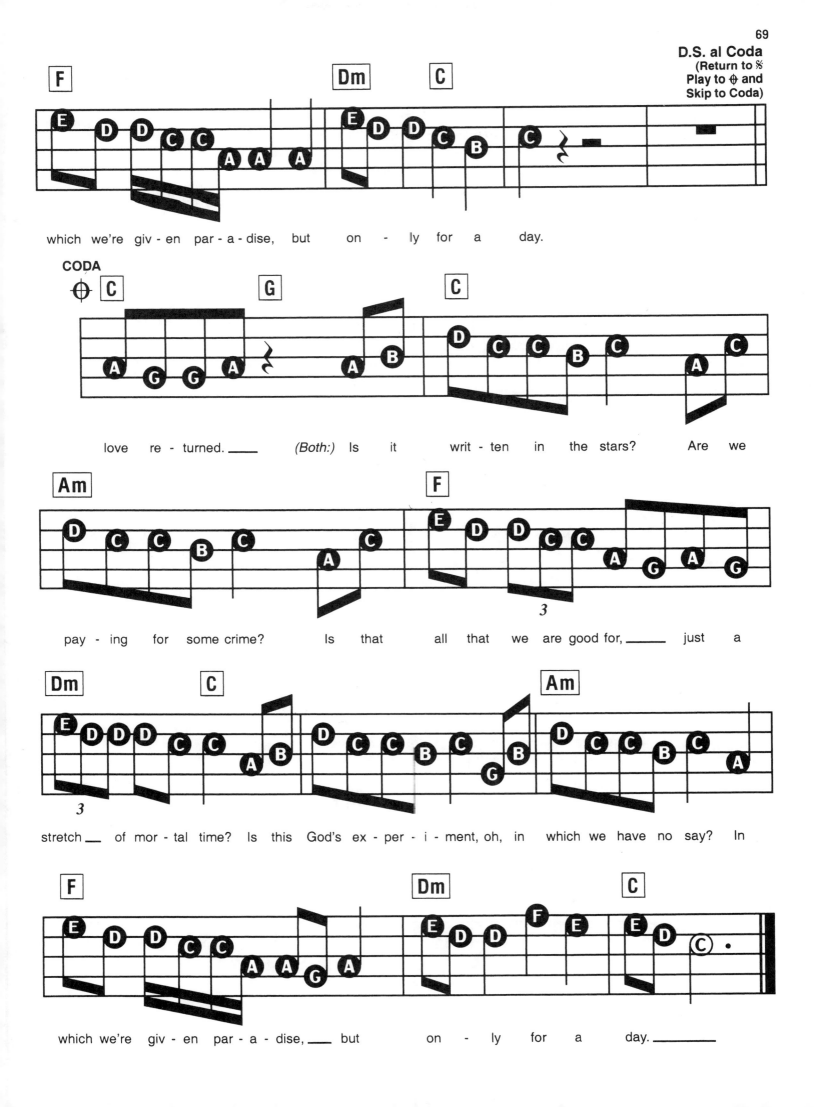

You Can Make History
(Young Again)

Registration 2
Rhythm: 8-Beat or Pop

Words and Music by Elton John
and Bernie Taupin

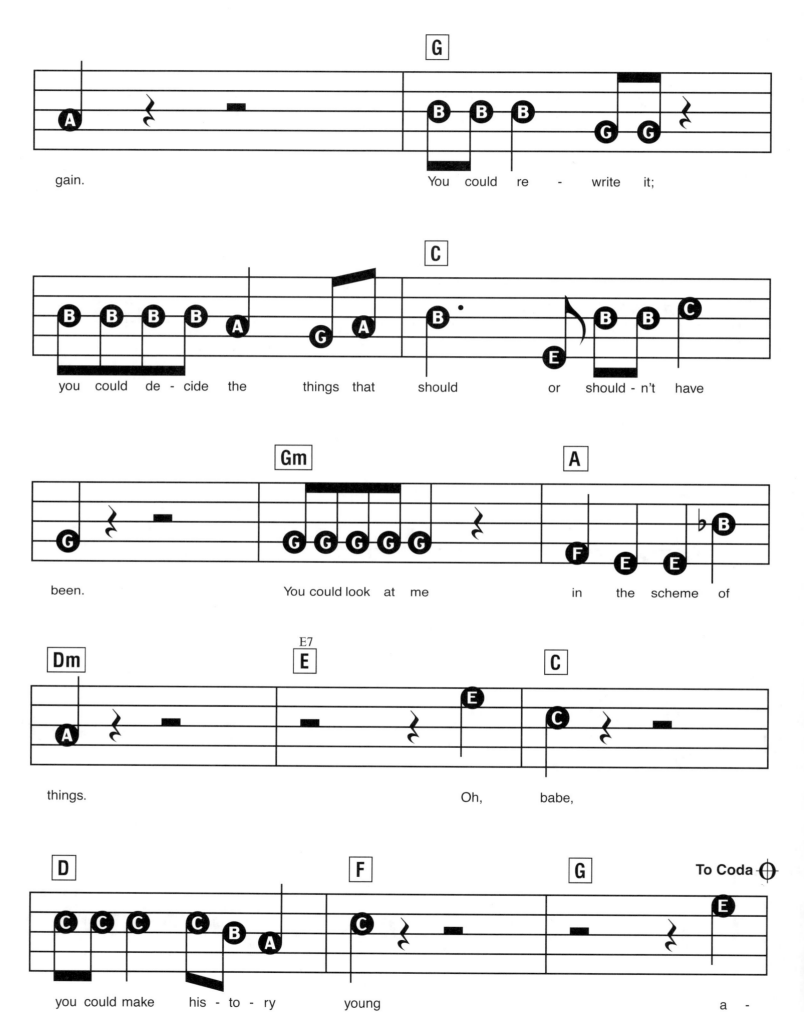

73

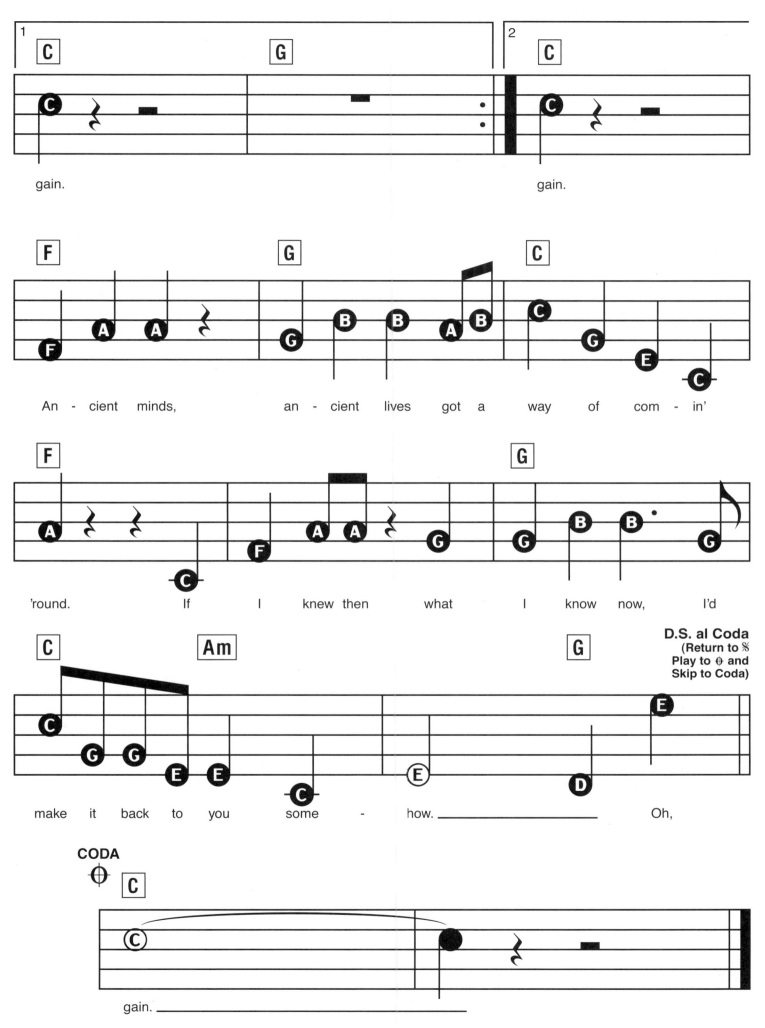

Your Song

Registration 3
Rhythm: Ballad or Pops

Words and Music by Elton John
and Bernie Taupin

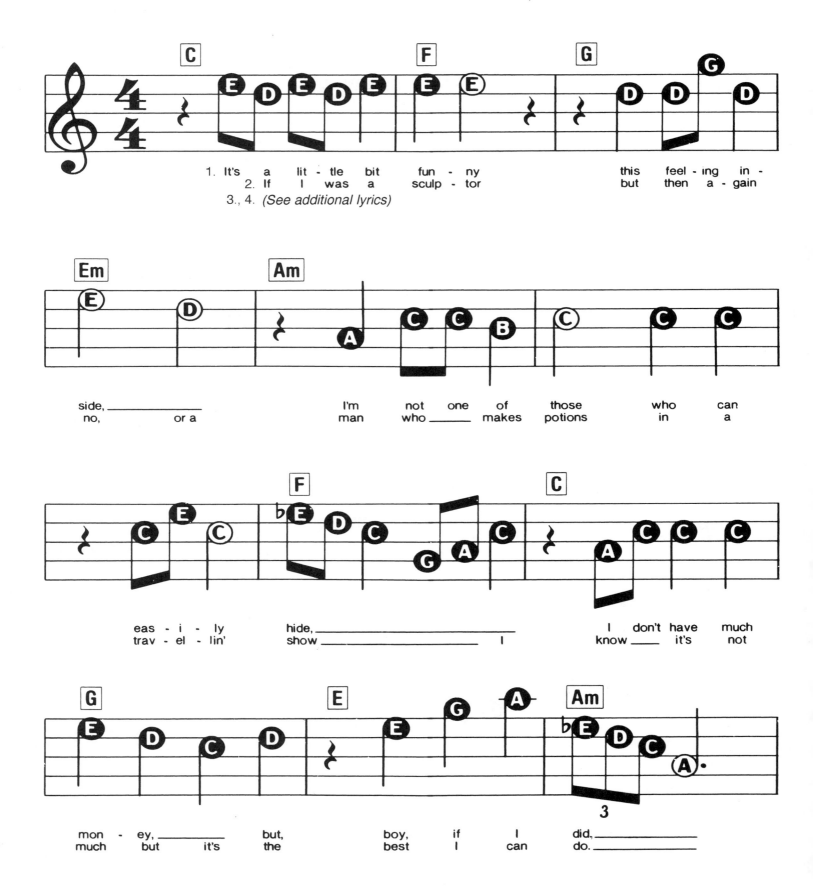

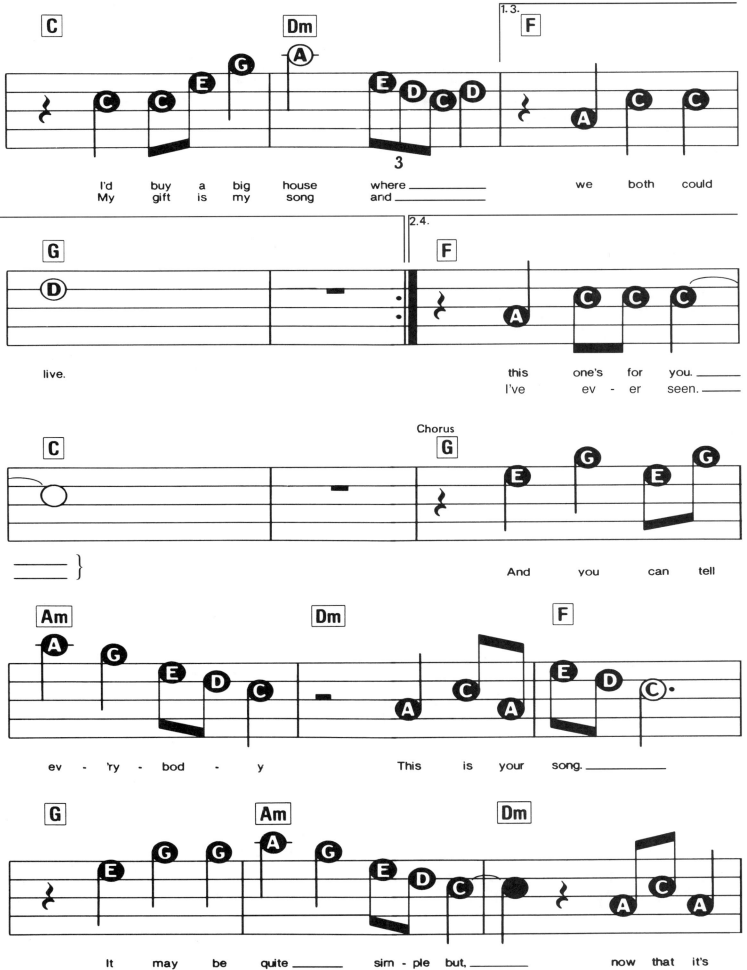

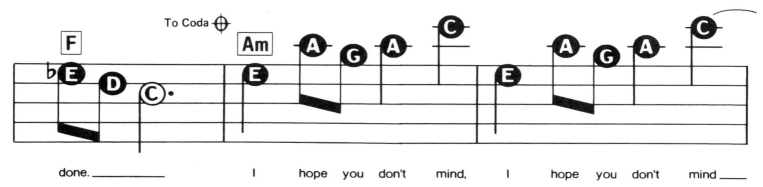

done. _____ I hope you don't mind, I hope you don't mind ____

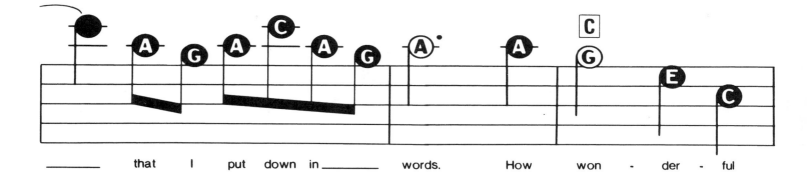

_____ that I put down in _____ words. How won - der - ful

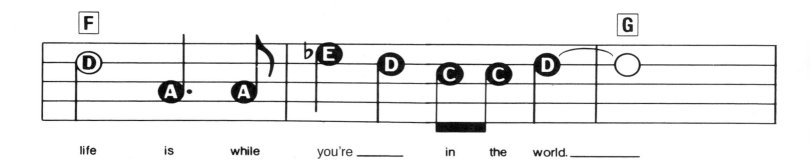

life is while you're _____ in the world. _____

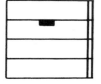

D.C. al Coda
(Return to beginning, take 3rd & 4th endings, Play till ⊕ and skip to Coda)

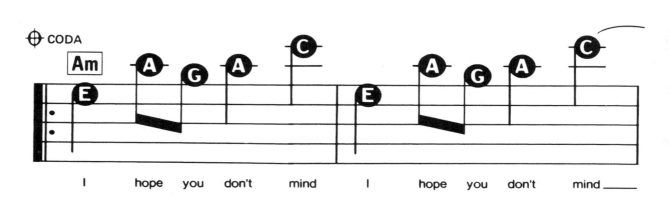

I hope you don't mind I hope you don't mind ____

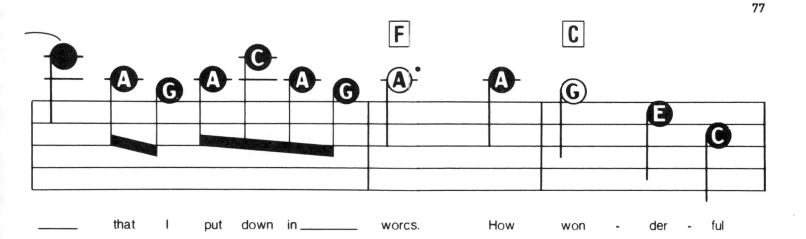

_____ that I put down in _____ words. How won - der - ful

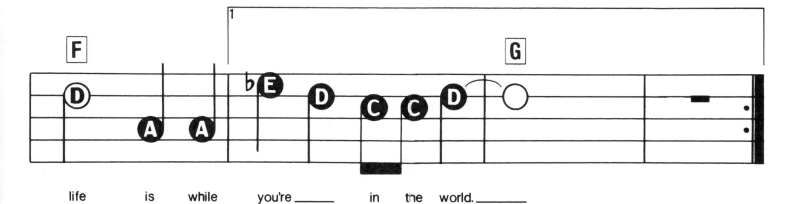

1

life is while you're _____ in the world. _____

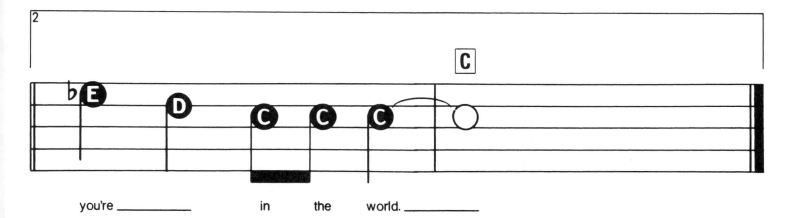

2

you're _____ in the world. _____

Additional Lyrics

3. I sat on the roof and kicked off the moss.
   well a few of the verses, well they've got me quite cross,
   But the sun's been quite kind while I wrote this song,
   It's for people like you that keep it turned on.

4. So excuse me forgetting but these things I do
   You see I've forgotten if they're green or they're blue,
   Anyway the thing is what I really mean
   Yours are the sweetest eyes I've ever seen.
   Chorus

You Gotta Love Someone
featured in the Paramount Motion Picture DAYS OF THUNDER

Registration 4
Rhythm: Rock or 8-Beat

Words and Music by Elton John
and Bernie Taupin

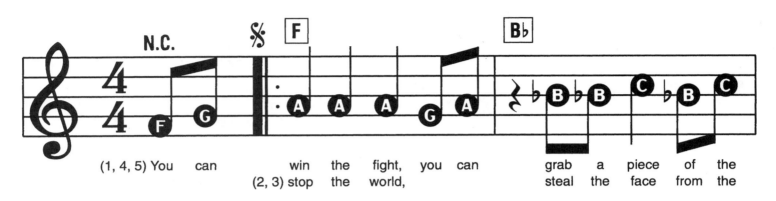

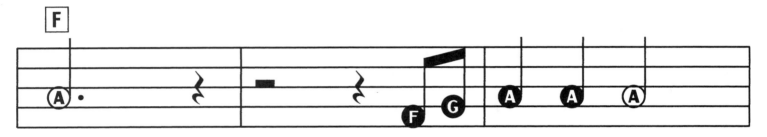

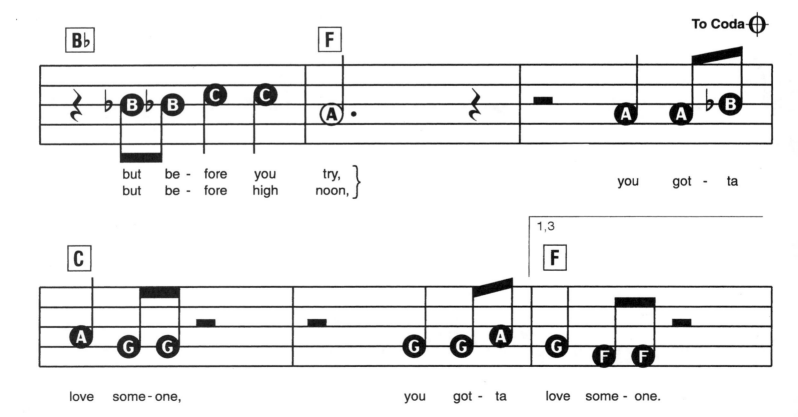

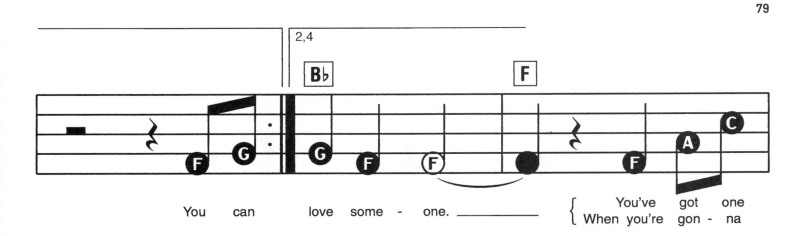

You can love some - one. _____ { You've got one
                                  { When you're gon - na

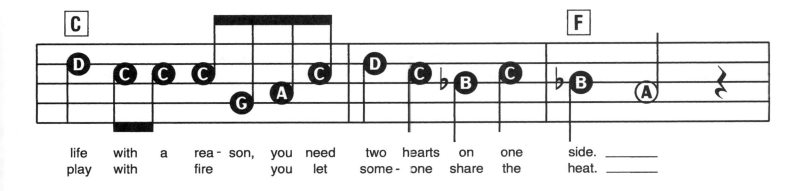

life with a rea - son, you need two hearts on one side. _____
play with fire you let some - one share the heat. _____

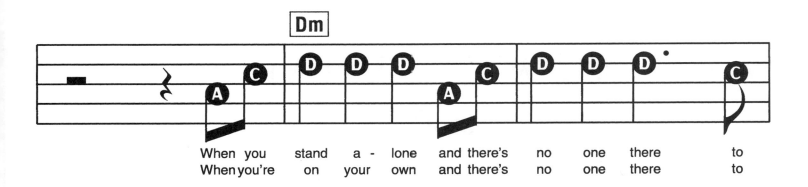

When you stand a - lone and there's no one there to
When you're on your own and there's no one there to

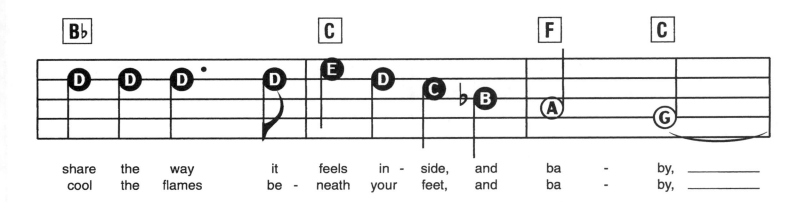

share the way it feels in - side, and ba - by, _____
cool the flames be - neath your feet, and ba - by, _____

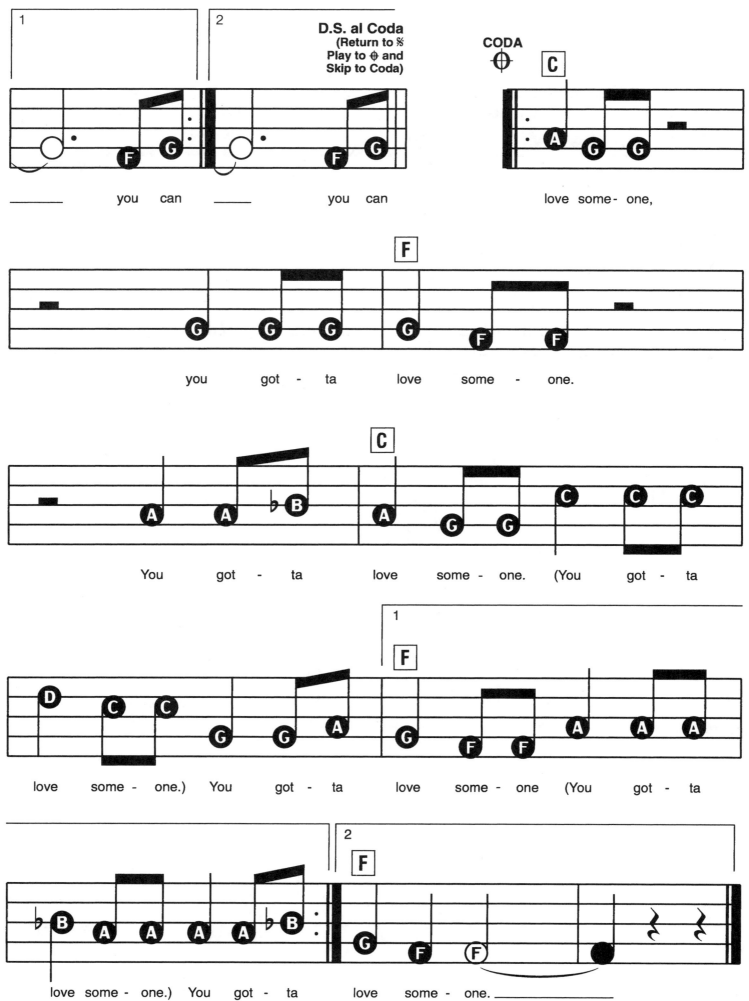